# Fit-For-Purpose Leadership #6

## Special Edition

**LEADERSHIPGIGS**

**Fit For Purpose Leadership 6**

Copyright 2020 Wallen Martin

First published in April 2020

Martin & Wallen (UK)

www.writingmatterspublishing.com

ISBN 979-8-639451-85-0 (Pbk)

Disclaimer: *Fit For Purpose Leadership 6* is intended for information and education purposes only. This book does not constitute specific advice unique to your situation. **PLEASE NOTE: This book does NOT this book contain medical, clinical, treatment or pharmaceutical advice.**

The views and opinions expressed in this book are those of the authors and do not reflect those of the Publisher and Resellers, who accept no responsibility for loss, damage or injury to persons or their belongings as a direct or indirect result of reading this book.

All people mentioned in case studies have been used with permission, and/or have had names, genders, industries and personal details altered to protect client confidentiality. Any resemblance to persons living or dead is purely coincidental.

To the best of our knowledge, the Publisher and Authors have complied with fair usage. The Publisher will be glad to rectify all future editions if omissions are bought to their attention.

# Contents

# Welcome To A Very Special Edition Of Fit For Purpose Leadership

## Andrew Priestley (Editor)

There is a rule in copywriting: avoid the exact date because it dates the story. But in this case, the dating is historic, significant and relevant.

At the time of publishing, the world - deemed by the World Health Organisation (WHO) - is in the grip of the coronavirus pandemic (COVID-19). The planet has literally shut down. It has come to a standstill.

For the first time in 30 years there Is no smog on the Himalayas, petrol prices are at a 30 year low, Governments are reeling at the pace of this pandemic, High Street commerce has ground to a halt, there is a shortage of toilet paper, panic buying, domestic violence is at an all time high … and yet never before have we seen such global collaboration, communication and cooperation to cope with an united invisible enemy.

Never before was the saying truer: unless everyone wins, no-one wins.

When I was kid growing up the threat of world domination was coming from outer space in the form of monsters. Think *War of the Worlds, It Came From Outer Space, Independence Day.*

This threat comes in the form of a protein - transmitted by

coughing, sneezing and even breathing; or from contacting surfaces where this protein can live for up to 12-24 hours - that infects the lungs with a respiratory pneumonia. So virulent, it has shut the entire globe down.

The only reference point we have is the Spanish Flu of 1918-1920 which claimed the lives of up to 50 million people.

So how to we cope with a pandemic? How we cope is driven by leadership.

According to Neil R Hintze[1] (2008) in *First Responder Problem Solving and Decision Making In Today's Asymmetrical Environment* first responders confront a common challenge, namely the lack of exposure to and experience with asymmetric threats (i.e., terrorism and natural disasters) in training venues that would enable them to develop familiarity with a novel situation such as a global pandemic.

Despite a tsunami of literature on expert versus novice decision making, situation awareness, recognition-primed decision making, and scenario-based learning there are few scenario-based exercises that provide insight and plausible remedies regarding the current asymmetric threat in the form of recommendations to enhance the first responder's ability to develop good situational awareness and decision making.

Right now we are on a steep learning curve; and a race against time.

Naturalistic decision making is the way individuals use their experience to solve problems in real-world settings. They identify the situation and take action during times of uncertainty.

Decision-making theorist Gary Klein[2] believes that today's first responders often use their power of intuition when problem solving in their respective lines of work. They have to — time is a rare commodity at a fire, in an emergency room, or at a crime scene. Experienced firefighters, nurses, and police officers exhibit expert problem-solving skills every day in their emergency response roles.

In fact they use Recognition-Primed Decision-Making (RPD) strategies. Recognition in this case relies on patterns, pattern matching, cue recognition, trail and error, mental simulations and behavioural models. Basically, we observe for similarities that identify critical situational markers. Then mental models can be used to navigate forward as in-stock decision-making resources.

From this we develop standard operating procedures (SOPs). Essentially, what fills manuals follows a proven methodology:

- ID the problem
- Gather data
- Develop a criteria
- Generate possible solutions
- Analyse potential solutions
- Compare possible solutions
- Make and implement the decision.

Basically, under normal conditions, the decision making structure is symmetrical: we know what it is and how to deal with it.

Asymmetrical events are the opposite: we don't know how this will play out and therefore what we need to do. Oddly, despite extreme levels of uncertainty, we are still managing.

Right now we are following a standard operating procedure for a pandemic based on what we have learned form recent and long past scenarios. The Spanish Flu. The SARS virus.

What makes COVID-19 different to The Spanish Flu pandemic is instant global communication, global political cooperation, a medical infrastructure that despite being overwhelmed is heroically resilient and responsive, backed by the collaborative intention of the medical world racing to find a vaccination.

Our response to natural disasters and hostile threats pretty much applies to localised events, regardless of how devastating they are.

This is different.

This is a global, hostile, all-pervasive threat that is no respecter of gender, race, religion, age or status. The known response is to minimise and contain the damage. This works if you recognise the threat and respond. The primary strategy is lock down. Stay at home. And suddenly that's what billions of people are now doing.

But this has caused unprecedented and major disruptions to everyday life. Commerce has all but ground to halt. In some countries people are technically under house arrest.

Dealing with this level of disruption calls for very unique style of leadership.

I cannot think of time other than world wars when there was a greater need for grounded leadership across every aspect of short term day to day and the long term long range view.

While crisis management almost begs the need for martial law with the intention of preserving life, we are dealing with an issues that requires people to fail fast, adjust and pivot.

Nowhere do we see this more than in business.

In ten very short days we realised we could work from home. In the best-seller *#RemoteWorking* we discovered that it is possible to prosper from the comfort of the kitchen table. This is giving the world of commerce a literal pause for thought.

We are seeing entire companies pivot their products, services and business models so dramatically that the need to return to am physical workplace is no longer necessary.

What has become glaringly obvious is how people perform under pressure. The efficacy of leaders - or the lack of it - is now highly visible. Forced into a primal corner we are no longer tolerant of leaders that posture and strut.

I hope this continues. Angela Merkel's address to Germany is a shining example of leadership that is empathetic, clear and non-patronising. By contrast other leaders have enraged us withs puerile, bloated and heavy handed rhetoric.

A glaring political anomaly is the lack of women leaders - an issue taken up by several of our contributors, and yet it seems the countries that have fared better, sooner are women-lead governments. Countries that have dawdled, stumbled and experienced heavy losses seem to be lead by men.

As always, those in lower socio-economic classes have fared the worst. Ironically, it is the lowliest paid workers that have been manning the frontlines of health care, essential services and support.

I am proud of this edition.

It is the most important book I have ever published. I doubt if I will ever experience history being made on a scale this large ever again - a once in a lifetime thing.

My grandmother lived through the Spanish Flu of 1918-1920. In her words, we only survived it by working together. Sadly in her opinion, the lessons of collaboration and respect and support were quickly forgotten as the world stabilised and focused on getting back to what was deemed normal.

In this case, I doubt that we will know what normal is for sometime to come. *RemoteWorking,* the dramatic shift to online and radical efficiency drives are already driving business reinvention.

Most of my comments relate to political leadership but I am most interested in and inspired by a conspicuous abundance of grass roots leadership that we are witnessing on the front-lines that is adaptive, fast and more equitable. Men and women working efficiently. Impeccably. Selflessly. I hope we remember their valour and stewardship.

Maybe we don't need normal leadership. Perhaps the rally cry is for impeccable abnormal leadership.

I am inspired by the calibre of authors from around the globe - leaders who have submitted well-considered thought pieces - and in record time.

I trust you are inspired to step into am leadership role - that will be much needed in this yet to be determined emerging future.


Andrew Priestley (Editor)

1.  Ref Hintze R.N. (2008) First Responder Problem Solving and Decision Making In Today's Asymmetrical Environment. Naval Postgraduate School.

2.  Source William Duggan, "Coup D'oeil: Strategic Intuition in Army Planning" (November 2005): 15. http://www.StrategicStudiesInstitute. army.mil/ [Accessed January 3, 2007].

# Leadership Strategies That Turn Defeat Into Victory

## Bob Hayward

My favourite quote is: *If you have come to help me you can go home again. But if you see my struggle as part of your own survival then perhaps we can work together.* The author was apparently an Australian aboriginal woman. I wish I knew her name.

Why listen to me? If you are reading this book in 2020, the world is in a tough place. Globally, our health and the economies are being ravaged by a pandemic.

I am not sitting in an ivory tower with all the answers. I am not right. Not perfect. Not here to help and go home. I am here to struggle through this tough time together with you. I started my first business in the 80s. Now seven successful businesses later, some of which grew and thrived during troubling times, there are some leadership lessons worth reflecting on. I am fighting to keep my own two businesses running and fighting hard to keep my client's businesses afloat. I'd rather thrive, of course who wouldn't. If I must just survive then so be it. Writing this chapter for you, helped me refocus on some leadership principles that enable me to get through previous tough times. I trust reading this chapter does the same for you.

General Bill Slim – have you heard of him? No, I hadn't either until recently. He should be a part of school history lessons and of all leadership development programmes. I was introduced to General Slim by Derek Peedell of Woodstock Law in Oxfordshire and I shall forever be grateful.

Earl Mountbatten, described Bill as "… the finest general World War II produced." Slim turned a badly mauled 14th British Army in Burma into a formidable force. He took command during the longest retreat in British military history. 900 miles through the Burmese jungle to India. 100 days and nights fighting through a jungle. He turned a disorderly panic into a controlled military withdrawal and subsequently stopped the Japanese advancing into India. He then refreshed his Army and went on the offensive ultimately defeating the much larger Japanese force. All of that on a shoestring budget because Burma was the least of Britain's concerns, the priority was the war in Europe. Slim's self-deprecating memoir, *Defeat into Victory*, is standard reading for all Military Leaders. One of the greatest books on military leadership ever written, it is also one of the best leadership books ever written. Read it.

On taking command he concluded that he had to solve three major problems: *health, supply* and *morale*. Interesting parallel to 2020. These same three things impact every country, probably every business and sadly most of us.

- **Leadership strategies**: Work out the smallest number of problems you must solve to create the biggest positive impact. Apply 80/20 Pareto rule. Reduce the number of variables and control the controllables.

Supply was a problem of weather, terrain and distance. Slim developed the revolutionary technique of air-land supply, enabling his army to march through trackless jungles properly supplied, armed and well informed – all by aircraft.

- **Leadership strategies:** Leverage your team, or network, and everyone's knowledge, intuition, creativity and skill to find a disruptive solution. Think outside of the box. Try the elegant and unconventional. Go bold. As Bill said, "When you cannot make up your mind which of two evenly balanced courses of action you should take, choose the bolder."

On health, he enforced practical application of the latest medical research for everyone. This included everyone taking malaria tablets, which soldiers hated because rumours suggested they made you sterile. Slim sacked three Senior Officers for not enforcing the malaria tablet regime. Declaring afterwards, 'by then the rest had got my meaning.' Slim defined leadership as: the projection of personality. It is that combination of persuasion, compulsion, and example that makes people do what you want them to do."

- **Leadership strategies:** The values, behavioural standards and fundamental business principles that you hold dear must be sacrosanct. Live by them yourself and compel your whole organisation to. Recruit for cultural fit, attitude and intelligence; not experience or skill. Use an iron fist in a velvet glove.
  Be quick, rigorous and crystal clear when people step out outside these values and principles while still being supportive.
  Create a non-blame culture that encourages learning from errors, to take calculated risks and to be bold. Adaptability, innovation and flexibility are created from fostering energy, and supporting a culture founded on trust and confidence. Put those that slip up on a development programme, if they change, good. If after three attempts they don't – change them for someone new.
  You can carry a few walking wounded during tough times.
  What you cannot carry, even in good times, is someone who sets themselves apart from your key values and principles.

Slim believed that integrity is central to leadership: "Integrity should not be so much a quality of itself as the element in which all of the others live and are active, as fish exist and move in the water. Integrity is a combination of the virtues of being honest with all men and of unselfishness, thinking of others, the people we lead, before ourselves."

At one critical point during the jungle retreat Slim came across a group of soldiers collapsed, exhausted, in a clearing. In a separate clearing nearby, he found the officers making themselves a proper camp for the night. While they were just as exhausted as their men, Slim explained to the officers that was not an excuse, "Officers are here to lead. I tell you, therefore, as officers, that you will neither eat, nor drink, nor sleep, nor smoke, nor even sit down until you have personally seen that your men have done those things. If you will do this for them, they will follow you to the end of the world. And, if you do not, I will break you."

In describing the British soldier: "Almost all soldiers are fundamentally the same. Germans, Russians, Frenchmen, perhaps even Italians. But the British Tommy generally manages to go on five minutes longer than his opposite number. You have to get that five minutes overtime out of your men. And, the only way to get it is by giving them the whole of your own time and thought and care. If you do this. they will never let you down."

- **Leadership strategies:** You are only an authentic leader, if you have willing followers. If no one is following you are not leading. You must bring people with you. Discretionary effort is everything. That extra five minutes Slim describes gives you 200% higher performance levels and stunning results. Paying someone a wage means you merely get hands and feet in return, some of the time. You cannot buy the head and the heart that underpin the discretionary effort, you must earn them as a leader.

*The Five Dysfunctions of a Team* is a must-read book by Patrick Lencioni. In it he says, "If you could get all the people in an organisation rowing in the same direction, you could dominate any industry, in any market, against any competition, at any time. Not finance. Not strategy. Not technology. It is teamwork that remains the ultimate competitive advantage, both because it is so powerful and so rare."

During that jungle retreat, Slim learned a gruesome lesson: in war, there are no non-combatants. His headquarter staff, clerks and cooks had to fight the Japanese as well or their command posts would have been overrun. Slim decided that every soldier had to be a rifleman. Even the cooks had to train and qualify with every type of weapon the army had. Whenever Slim was forced to put his front-line troops on half rations, he did the same to his headquarters staff.

- **Leadership strategies:** Teams start together and finish together, they do not leave anyone behind. Team means I look after myself and my job well enough that I have the capacity to also look after you if needed. Team means you look after yourself and your job well enough that if needed you can look after me. In business train each job three people deep. Especially in tough times you need a flexible workforce. Ensure each key job can be adequately handled by at least three different people. And everyone must be involved in sales and customer service – everyone is a rifleman. Work through the five dysfunctions of a team. Encourage people to use the principles from Stephen Covey's book *The Speed of Trust*. Teach people Empathy Styles, the temperament style indicator, probably the best tool for improving your emotional intelligence. Train people to use the tools and skills from *Crucial Conversations* by Switzler, Grenny, and McMillan.

In tough times leaders must put a great deal into lifting morale. Slim did. He decided there were three foundation stones to morale that he could affect: *material, intellectual* and *spiritual*.

From a material perspective he believed that a soldier must feel he gets a fair deal from his commanders and the army. He must, as far as possible in the situation, be given honest answers to questions and the truth behind problems; the best weapons and equipment for his task, and that his working conditions must be as good as they can be.

Intellectually, a soldier must be convinced that the goal, however tough, and the plan of action, however difficult must be doable. That every small win will be celebrated.

Communication must be accurate and flow up and down fast. He must see the organisation demonstrate efficiency. And that it provides the best equipment and supplies possible given the circumstances.

He must have confidence in his leaders. Only the best get that incredible responsibility. Those leaders must share the same dangers and hardships, so a soldier knows whatever he is called upon to do or suffer will not be asked of lightly.

Spiritually, there must be a great and noble goal. What Jim Collins in *Good to Great* calls the BHAG, the *Big Hairy Audacious Goal*. Its achievement must be vitally important, it must have meaning. The method of achievement must be active and aggressive, and the soldier must feel that he matters and what he does helps the attainment of the goal.

- **Leadership strategies:** Leadership has the biggest impact on the culture of a team, and culture has the biggest impact on performance. While we each have different motivational drives to those around us, the leader helps create the environment within which each team member can be motivated. Tough times are when leaders need to engage, listen and support the most. Tough times are when you must remember the constant is activity. Opportunities come and go. Results come and go. It is the soil of the farm that converts the seeds into crops that can be harvested. The farm is the constant. Success is about doing the right things often enough and well enough. Leaders must make sure people know what those right things are. To ensure they are done at the right frequency and at the right quality.

Writing this chapter for you, helped me refocus on some leadership principles that enable me to get through previous tough times. I trust reading this chapter has done the same for you.

And remember, like Winston Churchill said, "Never, never, never give up."

## About Bob Hayward

Bob Hayward, a Christian, a father to four, granddad to five (so far) and a Spurs fan; if you can cope with those facts then you will get on well with him.

He is a catalyst for change to those who want a business breakthrough, a best-selling author and popular international speaker. Having started seven businesses, and is still running two, he now loves using his experience and the skills developed along the way to make growth happen for others - sometimes as a Non-Executive Director, or a Growth Consultant or as a Senior Executive Coach.

He has designed and delivered numerous mission-critical internal communication initiatives, employee engagement projects and skill development programmes for companies like Vodafone, BMW, and Skype. Feedback on his work is high in both levels of delegate satisfaction and of tangible business improvements.

Bob has previously co-authored two Amazon Best Sellers:

- Persuade: How to persuade anyone about anything
- Remote Working: How to effectively and efficiently work from home in challenging times

Contact him at *https://www.linkedin.com/in/bobhayward/*

Read more from Bob *https://www.bemoreeffective.com/blog/*

# The Five Pillars Of Great Leadership: Showing Up As Your Best Self In Good Times And In Bad

## Alessandra Wall PhD

"What makes a great leader?"

Ask 500 people that same question and you would be surprised by how consistent their answers are. When you take the time to explore the *what* and *how* of great leadership you quickly realize that five fundamental principles emerge. These principles form what I call the Five Pillars of great leadership, and they are equally articulated by executives and managers, entrepreneurs and physicians, military personnel and even children.

In the best of times, a leader's ability to operate according to the Five Pillars is essential to engaging teams and communities, building stable and sound organizations, and providing a framework for strategic growth, innovation, and prosperity. During a crisis, the Five Pillars are crucial to the life, success, and survival of companies, communities, and individuals.

In the midst of the current pandemic and the inevitable ensuing economic downturn, leaders everywhere should become more familiar with the Five Pillars and strive to build the skills they lack, shore up the ones they have, and stay ever-aware of new opportunities to practice these skills.

# PILLAR I

## Great Leaders Are Value-Driven Strategic Thinkers

Great leaders think strategically. They have a long-term vision of what they and their organizations can achieve and a clear process for executing that vision. Both their objectives and their approach to leadership are driven by explicitly articulated core values. Those values are expressed through a set of defined principles of operation and engagement.

In psychology, we say that *what you think is who you are; your reality is defined by the beliefs and assumptions you hold.* Those beliefs shape your perception of events, your emotional response, and your choice of actions. The same holds true for a leader's core values. They are deeply-rooted assumptions and beliefs that fundamentally shape how they perceive and respond to events. When a leader is clear about who she is, what matters to her, and how she wants to interface with the world, she creates a strong and stable framework for decision making.

Clearly articulated core values and principles provide a road map for decision making especially in unpredictable or ambiguous situations. In a climate of uncertainty and under extreme stress it is easy to give in to fear and operate reactively, shifting objectives, strategies, and approaches with every new turn of events and every new downturn of events. The leader who uses value-driven strategic thinking has established a framework to respond to circumstances calmly, strategically and proactively. She can shield her teams from the impact of erratic shifts and provide stability and predictability in an unpredictable climate, which in turn builds trust and confidence.

# PILLAR II

## Great Leaders Are Team-Focused

Great leaders understand that teams are not just a collection of individuals operating independently but an interwoven collective of people, each with unique skills, personalities, and assets that come together to form a greater unit. Great leaders work to educate, elevate, and empower their teams to be as successful as possible. They understand the human dynamics of a team and work to facilitate collaboration and address the inevitable conflict that comes when you ask many people to work as one. A great leader knows to give the team credit where credit is due, and takes accountability when the team falls short or fails.

Under stress, our ability to think strategically, process subtle or complex cues, and respond with nuance and consideration is undermined. What that means - both at an individual and a team level - is that we are more prone to respond reactively, become irritable, and feel overwhelmed and confused by information. This isn't due to a failing of the individual but to how our brains adapt to stress. When anxious, a human's prefrontal cortex - the part of our brain that processes information, plans, and thinks strategically - is compromised. A team-focused leader knows his people and their dynamics well enough to anticipate the tensions and changes that will arise due to stress during a crisis. He will be better equipped to navigate conflict, have difficult conversations, and help his team to shift expectations and adapt to critical circumstances.

## PILLAR III

### Great Leaders Champion Individuals

In addition to being team-focused, great leaders are individuals champions. They take the time to know and understand the people who work for them. They seek and groom talent. They are not threatened by the excellence of those under them but excited by the opportunity to help others grow, thrive, and move up all proverbial ladders. Great leaders are mentors and sponsors. They prepare their best and their brightest to one day step into their shoes or leave the nest. They understand that the success of those who serve them is the greatest testament to their leadership skills.

In times of crisis, leaders rely heavily on their best and brightest to move operations along, keep teams afloat, and drive productivity and innovation when others can't. A true individual champion will know who these people are. She will understand how best to leverage their skills to both support the organization and give the individual a chance to shine and articulate their value in the midst of a crisis. She will have their trust. This relationship is central to the health of the organizations, but also to the individual teams that rely not only on the leader but also on these leaders-in-the-making to navigate a crisis.

## PILLAR IV

### Great Leaders Lead

Great leaders lead; they proverbially and sometimes literally are the first into battle and the last ones out of a burning building. They step up in hard times and are the first to sacrifice when resources are limited. They are willing to sit down to difficult conversations and face conflict even when it's uncomfortable. They will make unpopular choices when those choices are best for the organization or the team. They have great expectations, and they model the behaviors they expect from others. They are decisive and direct, and they take ownership of their role as decision-maker.

The leader who leads is a hero during a crisis. Because he is decisive, because he can put the needs of others above his own discomfort, and because he communicates openly and honestly, those operating under him know that he can be counted on. A great leader understands what Uncle Ben famously said to Peter Parker in the *Spiderman* comics, that with great power comes great responsibility- that responsibility is his to take.

## PILLAR V

### Great Leaders Demonstrate Great Character

Coming full circle, great leaders have great personal character. It's that character that informs the core values and principles they operate from, and it is at the foundation of what makes a great leader trustworthy. When you ask people about these characteristics they talk of honesty, authenticity, openness, and vulnerability. They share stories about leaders who take ownership and demonstrate accountability, who voice their limitations but know their strengths and assets. They speak of leaders who are self-aware, humble, and responsive.

Crises bring out the best and the worst in people. It's why we are so awed by the CEO who gives up her annual salary to keep her base employed, and why we feel so much antagonism towards the manager who pressures her team to work harder and longer hours under the threat (implied or stated) of unemployment. Leaders with great character are more often than not going to be the ones showing up at their best under pressure, and even if/when they slip, we will forgive them because we know that at baseline they have the foundations of greatness.

### Leadership Is A Skill

Leadership is a skill. Like all skills, some are naturally born more talented, but everyone needs to learn, practice, and perfect if they want to one day become a great leader. The Five Pillars model provides a simple framework for understanding which qualities are most relevant and meaningful to those you have the privilege of leading. Think about the best and the worst leaders you have had to operate under, compare their qualities to the Five Pillars and it easy to see how fundamental these qualities are. In times of crisis, what people need most is clarity, confidence, and compassion. Leaders who operate according to the Five Principles naturally provide those things. It's our responsibility as leaders to honestly evaluate our practices, step up, and show up better.

## About Dr Alessandra Wall

Dr. Alessandra Wall is a licensed clinical psychologist and leadership coach who specializes in helping women secure the careers and success they've earned.

She specializes in helping smart, professional women find their voices, show up more confidently, and succeed on their own terms. Her mission is to advocate for and act as an ally for women who want to make their mark, be heard, and succeed professionally, and support organizations that genuinely strive to retain and elevate these exceptional women.

Dr. Wall has been in private practice in San Diego since 2007, she founded Life in Focus Coaching in 2013 to better support the women she was working with. She received her Bachelor of Arts in psychology (Cum Laude) from Duke University and her Doctorate of Philosophy in clinical psychology from the University of Texas Southwestern Medical Center.

*www.lifeinfocussd.com*

*https://www.linkedin.com/in/dralessandrawall/*

# Calm In The Eye Of The Storm

## Richard Bellars

*"The only safe ship in a storm is leadership." ~ Faye Wattleton*

"ALL HANDS ON DECK!" The huge storm we had seen on the horizon, and thought had passed, had circled back, slap bang on top of us. I looked back up to the main ship. Lightning flashed horizontally back and forth across swirling, angry clouds, silhouetting the ship's outline, rain lashing down ... and there I was, barefoot, being tossed around in the small metal dinghy to secure it alongside a ferro-cement ship with three metal masts. It suddenly hit me this was not a good place to be!

I was in terrified awe, at the mercy of Nature.

Then it came. A profound wave of calm. From somewhere within. I could see chaos and panic on board. Yet I couldn't have felt more alive, live or die, tiny and insignificant, yet also connected to something far, far greater. I felt humble, grateful, peaceful even. Time slowed. Time expanded. Feeling calm, exhilarated, present, I rejoined the main deck to offer encouragement, assistance and any know-how to my fellow crew. We secured the ship and whatever hadn't been blown away or cut loose to save essentials from damage, then rode out the storm on our shared floating home, feeling deep relief and gratitude, including for the many lessons and reminders.

This memory of 'inner journey through outer adventure' evokes many emotions and lessons relevant to the current combination of global pandemic and climate crisis. For sure, the daily unfolding of the pandemic is far more intense and extreme for many, while also affecting every one of us on our shared planet; but certain principles and practices are consistently applicable.

So, please pause ... breathe ... with a longer exhale than normal ... How are you? How are you *really*? Notice what you are feeling... Maybe even put this book down and really give yourself a moment of your own attention, just for a moment. Be with what you feel.

Uncertainty? Anxiety? Excitement? Optimism? There are many levels of and responses to fear being felt right now. Grief also, at the loss of loved ones, of identities, jobs and livelihoods, of social connection, of simple ways of life we maybe took for granted ... all of which can build like an emotional tidal wave!

Through delivering coaching-based transition programmes for injured military veterans (a humbling privilege via the phenomenal UK charity *Help For Heroes*), I am reminded how the spectrum of mental health issues is the body system's natural response to threat. The more intense the threatening situation, the greater the response. This is regardless of whether the threat is physical or emotional, real or perceived as real (even imagined). The overriding emotions are fear and grief. Sound familiar to where we find ourselves today? Fear and grief are human, emotional responses to threat and loss. How we feel is not wrong. The question is what do you choose to do with the messages your system is giving you.

One of the models we use with the veterans is Gilbert's *Three Circles of Emotional Regulation*[1] - a.k.a *Threat, Drive, Soothe* – all key brain functions that each play their vital role in keeping us alive, healthy and resilient, when calibrating together in dynamic balance in any situation.

### Threat function

Threat function constantly scans for risk to our survival needs, which could be extreme or as simple as recognising thirst, hunger and the need to sleep/rest/replenish. The principle hormone released into the system is cortisol.

### Drive function

Drive function wants to perform, achieve and accomplish. The principle hormone is serotonin.

### Soothe function

Soothe function wants to slow down, rest, digest, rebalance the whole system; includes feeling safe, self care, compassion, connection/bonding and empathy. The principle hormone is oxytocin. A healthy 'Soothe' function calms an overstimulated 'Threat' that otherwise makes us hyper-vigilant, and an over-stimulated 'Drive' that can otherwise leads to burnout.

This awareness can help any human, firstly, with understanding and normalising feelings, emotions and behaviours, then with giving a greater sense of choice in how to rebalance. This is moving from 'reactive' to 'creative' - same letters, different words depending on the position from which we 'c' things. (See?)

'Soothe' can also be called 'active recovery' - having daily awareness, tools and practices to reset in any moment or situation. As such, as leaders all, how can we choose to respond consciously and effectively in our current context?

- **Acknowledgement:** feel the fear in your body, name it if you can – once you acknowledge a fear, that 'tight' energy starts to move, to loosen and release its grip. As the saying goes, 'What we resist will persist; but what we shine a light on goes away'.

- **Normalisation:** you're a human being and it's totally OK to feel what you're feeling. Considering this for yourself will nurture empathy for others. Let's stop giving ourselves a hard time for what we didn't do / can't do, have greater compassion for ourselves and others, and refocus our attention on what we can do; this may well include what we forgot we are capable of ... or that we could now find out by having a go.  By showing up and 'being human', with the empathy of an open heart and mind, then we can step into being more forward-facing, imaginative and practical in approaching whatever is going on.

- **Motivation**: our fears are telling us, in no uncertain terms, what we don't want; AND, if we listen, they can also point us, with focus, to what we DO want.  To access this guidance, we can ask ourselves empowering questions (Where am I in this moment? What do I need to let go of? What is essential to be able to move forward? What could be the highest good to come of this? What would be the single most effective next action?) to shift ourselves to more resourceful states ... of courage, possibility, innovation, determination, resilience, collaboration, compassion ... I could go on, because human beings can be extra-ordinary when they choose to be!

- **Emotional Contagion:** this is the transfer of emotions and moods between people and back again.  Perpetuating fear risks being even more of a pandemic than the actual pandemic, both now and possibly later, if there are mass emotional knock-on effects.  Unless we choose and act otherwise.  Positive emotional contagion can be spread by leaders authentically demonstrating empathy, determination, clear communication, calm co ordination and collaboration towards clear shared goals, encouraging and boosting morale and cohesion along the way.

This is where calm is a 'superpower' for leadership.

As well as the 'Soothe' effect for rebalancing the Emotional Regulatory System, calmness creates space for perspective.  Perspective offers the chance to see and sense differently what is happening and create a shift in attitude.  That shift in attitude can transform threat into challenges we can act on, the best we can.  This growth mindset sees challenge as opportunity.

With practice, pause and perspective change how we see and experience things.  Even when we haven't chosen a situation, we can choose how we respond.  Then what we are seeing and experiencing changes.  The more we practice, the more we move from unconscious reaction to conscious choice.

With small steps to integrate this into daily practise, the stronger and more natural this will become.

We see this in the daily acts of courage by front-line health and support staff, to show up to do their jobs knowing their own lives could be at risk. We are also hearing of countless acts of kindness, generosity, innovation, creativity, compassion and care in our communities across the globe.

I love that the word 'courage' come from the French word 'coeur', meaning heart. In response to this global challenge, we are also witnessing a global outpouring of love, compassion and gratitude. Wherever there is love, fear melts away. If love feels too much of a stretch, let us start with compassion and gratitude.

This is where compassion can become the new currency and imperative for community and future business as social business: to support and sustain self, other and planet, without the need for a crisis as catalyst.

This intensely challenging and disruptive time will be a great cleanser that could herald a new era of whole systems collaboration, innovation and enterprise for well-being and sustainability. With the individual and collective will to be and do things differently, this local/global challenge could be the initiation to transform our old paradigm of 'ME' to one of 'WE'. Scharmer and Kaufer describe this as moving "from ego system to eco-system".[2] We are remembering we ARE all already inter-connected.

Will we have the will to be and do differently, through heart-felt courage to love and act fearlessly and co-create with kindness? I believe so. I believe in you. I believe in us. And I believe this is already happening, in the moments and places that we give our highest intention and attention.

1.  Gilbert, P. (2009). The Compassionate Mind: A New Approach To Life's Challenges. London: Constable & Robinson

2.  Scharmer, O. & Kaufer, K. (2013). Leading from the Emerging Future: From Ego-System to Eco-System Economies. San Francisco: Berrett-Koehler Publishers Inc.

## About Richard Bellars

Richard Bellars supports 'Evolving Leadership' through facilitation, coaching and mentoring. For more than a decade he has delivered experiential learning and social change programmes in UK, Europe, Africa and Middle East for social entre- preneurs, women in business, leaders in conservation, and for injured veterans in transition.

His background includes corporate change management consulting and he speaks fluent French and Spanish. He has a passion for travel and has co-lead small groups on "open adventures of self-exploration" in remote parts of the world. He is an active Trustee of the London Sports Trust and a Fellow at the RSA (Royal Society for the encouragement of Arts, Manufactures and Commerce).

*LinkedIn: https://www.linkedin.com/in/richardbellars*

*Twitter: @richardbellars*

# Chief Empathy Officers (CEOs) Needed...

**Julia Felton**

We all find ourselves in a completely unexpected and unprecedented situation. As the world reels in the crisis of the global pandemic we are experiencing a situation where nearly every person in every country is in almost exactly the same situation. Not since the days of Sabre Tooth Tigers and Woolly Mammoths has humanity become the prey, instead of being the predator. Individuals are having to get accustomed to being in locked down, children are being home schooled and businesses are having to reinvent themselves to adjust to this new environment.

There is massive uncertainty in the world and this is leading to fear. As humans our basic instinct is to crave safety and security, and when these factors are taken away from us our brain's response it to go into fight, flight or freeze, in order to protect ourselves. We're seeing all these responses happening as people crave to get back to normality, to the safety they once knew. The tough reality though is that things will never be the same again. The world is going through a massive transformation. A metamorphosis that will see the old systems, structures and ways of working break and be replaced by new norms. And as when anything new births, there will be pain and hardship along the way. That's what we are experiencing right now with many people losing their incomes and struggling to survive, and others paying the ultimate sacrifice with their lives.

For leaders there is a new world emerging. One where the old paradigm of command and control will no longer serve us. We need leaders right now to step up and take the lead. To show us the way, but not in a self-serving way. Leaders are needed to provide safety and security at a time when many feel helpless and to lead us from chaos and confusion to clarity, confidence and certainty. Everyone is experiencing this crisis in different ways and as leaders we need to be empathetic to this. That is why now more than ever we need leaders to become the Chief Empathy Officer (CEO) of their business.

## So What Is Empathy?

Empathy is ability to put yourself in someone else's shoes and see, hear and feel the world through their eyes, ears and emotions. When a leader focuses on empathy and compassion before business performance team members feel a sense of safety, trust, empowerment and growth.

Empathy is a key attribute of Emotional Intelligence (EI), also know as Emotional Quotient (EQ), a concept developed by psychologist Daniel Goleman in 1995. Over the last decade we have increasingly seen EQ becoming a key requirement of leaders, so much so that the World Economic Forum, in their Future of Jobs Report, identified EQ as being in the top ten leadership skills needed to thrive in 2020.

It's a basic human need to feel understood but this is also how we connect, help, and support one another. If we can't recognise someone in pain, how can we support them? If we are unable to accept and empathise with our own emotions, it is difficult to be present to people around us. This is why empathy is crucial for our interconnectivity.

Empathy provides the gateway to human connection and right now we need leaders who engage in human to human communication and connection. Team members want to know they are being heard and that leaders really understand and appreciate what they are going through. When leaders display empathy they become relatable and this creates trust as team members and other stakeholders feel that the leader has their back and can really resonate with that is happening for them.

## So How Do Leaders Demonstrate Empathy To Others?

1. **Build Personal Connection** – empathetic leaders build social connection with their team members. They get to know people on a personal level including knowing their name, something about their family and hobbies. They display a genuine interest in the person. Without this a leader can have very little sense of how a situation will be impacting those around them as every person will experience the situation in a different way depending on their circumstances.

In the past leaders could build personal connection with "water cooler" chat and what Simon Sinek refers to as "eye-ball leadership" when you meet people face to face. Clearly the current crisis, with so many people working from home, has made this more difficult but not impossible. As a leader I'd encourage you to pick up the phone and check in with your team and other stakeholders. Ask them how they are doing and listen carefully to their responses.

2. **Active Listening** – at all times, but especially now, team members and other stakeholders want to know that they are being really listened to. There is a reason we have two ears and one mouth. So as a leader take the time to really listen to what is being said and importantly what is not being said. To do this, this means that you must be present in the moment and be able to hold a safe space so that others can open up about their own emotions and so that you can better understand their perspective of their experience.

3. **Be Compassionate** – knowing and understanding what others are going through enables you to be compassionate. It doesn't mean you have to agree to someone else's point of view, but rather by striving to understand it you can build deeper and more connected relationships.

**4. Speak The Truth** – as the Chief Empathy Officer you also have to be decisive and speak the truth. In times of crisis the reality is that people want to know the truth however hard that message is to hear. Knowing the truth and what is happening allows people to make choices and so feel more empowered.

This was a hard lesson I learnt when leading my team at Arthur Andersen through the Enron crisis some 20 years ago. As a novice leader I mistakenly thought I should protect my team from the bad news that all our jobs were potentially at threat of being made redundant. I did not want to worry them, but the lesson I learnt was that people would rather know the bad news so they could make their own decisions about how to react.

**5. Vulnerability** – great leaders build connection through human to human communication and showing how authentic and genuine they are. Leaders are human beings too and at this time we are all going through our own reactions to what is happening. Contrary to some thoughts I believe that showing vulnerability and your emotions does not make a leader seem weak, but rather makes leaders more relatable to others. It shows that the leader is human too and also going through their own journey of navigating these turbulent times.

During this crisis I have witnessed some great examples of leaders stepping up and taking on the mantel of Chief Empathy Officer. One example that particularly stands out to me is the video that Arne Sorenson, President and CEO of Marriott International, made for his entire team. In the video he demonstrates great leadership, empathy and vulnerability. He connects and relates to his team members appreciating the great work they have done and really understanding the challenges they are all going through, as many of the global workforce have been furloughed as a result of the global lockdown that has stopped travel. It is an authentic, heart-felt message that touched my heart and I'm not even a Marriott employee!.

Mr Sorenson even shares how he and Bill Marriott are

relinquishing their salaries for the remainder of the year whilst the rest of the Executive Team are taking a 50% cut in renumeration. This is a great example of a leader walking his talk and really getting into the shoes of his team members and empathising with the challenges they are going through.

What is all the more remarkable is that Arne Sorenson's compassion and empathy contrasts with other companies in the hospitality sector and the approach they have taken. In an industry whose success is driven by often minimum wage, zero contract hours employees, and that is struggling to find talent in a post Brexit world, never is there a more important time to keep your team members onside and support them, so they are available for you when the crisis abates. People remember bosses that care for them and I'm sure that the Marriott brand will thrive once again after this crisis. Whether that will be the case for others remains to be seen.

## The Business Benefits Of Displaying Empathy

As the business rule book has been thrown out of the window, and a new paradigm of leadership is emerging some leaders are struggling to adapt. Really stepping up and becoming the Chief Empathy Officer of their business means that they need to switch their strategy and course correct. Leaders have to become comfortable not being in control and be able to pivot at a moment's notice to ensure the success of the business. However, there is really compelling research as to why empathy is a key ingredient to fostering a positive workplace culture

The State of the Workplace Empathy study 2019 revealed that:

- 91% of CEO's believe that empathy is directly linked to financial performance

- 78% of employees work longer hours for more empathetic employers

- 82% of employees would consider leaving their job for more empathetic organisations

- 75% of employees state companies are more empathetic when they have diversity in leadership

So the business benefits are clear in terms of reduced turnover, increased productivity and profitability.  But more than that when you step up and become the Chief Empathy Officer of your business you start creating loyalty with your team members, customers and other stakeholders and that is something that is invaluable and will, beyond doubt, help companies thrive through this time of crisis and beyond.

## References

- Business Solver (2019) State of Work Place Empathy. www.business solver.com/resources/state-of-workplace-empathy

- Goleman, Daniel (1995) Emotional Intelligence: Why It Can Matter More Than IQ. Bantam

- Marriott International (2020) Tweet From Arne Sorenson https://twitter. com/marriottintl/status/1240639160148529160

- Sinek, Simon.  (2017) Leaders Eat Last: Why Some Teams Pull Together And Others Don't. New York: Penguin Group

- World Economic Forum (2016) The 10 Skills You Need To Thrive In The Fourth Industrial Revolution. www.weforum.org

## About Julia Felton

Julia Felton is a leadership development and team engagement strategist. She works with visionary founders, business owners and executives who are tired of the outdated ways of doing business and are looking for a new unconventional approach. One where they can create great impact and influence and whilst creating a great income.

Julia believes that business is a force for good and through designing purpose-driven businesses, leveraging the laws of nature, you can create businesses founded on the principles of connection, collaboration and contribution.

A former corporate executive Julia honed her leadership skills as an "intrapreneur" at Arthur Andersen and Deloitte creating and leading a global hospitality data research division that became the market leader in its field, before selling the business unit in 2008.

Julia is the author of two books *Unbridled Success* and *The Alchemy Of Change.* She is an international speaker and lives in Yorkshire with her herd of four horses.

*julia@businesshorsepower.com*

*www.businesshorsepower.com*

*www.linkedin.com/in/juliafelton*

# Trust – The New Bottomline

## Jim Hetherton

Whom do you trust - right now? Politicians? Scientist? Economists? The police? Yes, No, Maybe. Maybe not. Or not sure.

And if we don't trust them, why is that? Is it because we don't believe them; or they promise one thing, then do another? Or is it that they're just not very good.

Trust is a massive issue with the current pandemic. Governments are asking their citizens to change behaviours at an unprecedented level not seen since World War 2. Trust affects every element of society, mainly in the last ten years with the rise of social media, whether having to fact-check your Facebook or Twitter feeds or in listening to politicians.

In business, trust is taking a hit particularly when so many of us are working from home; as we ask ourselves: *how on earth did we get ourselves into this position?* Trust in 'brands' is down according to the world's largest PR firm Edelman. In their *2019 Trust Barometer:*

- More than 70 percent link purchase to considerations that historically were tied to trust in corporations, including supply chain, reputation, values, environmental impact and customer before profit.

- 53 percent of consumers agree that every brand has a responsibility to get involved in at least one social issue that does not directly impact its business.

Sadly, BP, for example, have become a business school case; Deepwater Horizon oil disaster in 2010 showed that highly paid managers seem to be only out for themselves.

"There is 'no evidence' that huge plumes of oil are suspended undersea," said BP. "The charges against us will hurt America," said Goldman. "The safety-related allegations against us are a big lie," said Massey. BP used a classic crisis management approach: deny, deflect, spin, and repeat. Rather than open up, they withheld information. They denigrated critics, blamed others and refused to answer pertinent questions or engage in meaningful debate. They hid behind the veneer of canned statements and corporate rhetoric, with the occasional blunder thrown in. Result - Share price fell from 650p to a low of 296p: a collapse of nearly 55%.

The differences between high and low trust organisations are palpable and measurable. It may well be that trust issues exist, but the good news is that trust is an issue that can be addressed. Here are some of the warning signs that trust is an issue in an organisation:

- Lots of checking up if people are really "Working from Home"
- Poor communications and lots of defensiveness.
- Intense political atmosphere with clear camps and parties
- An active, inaccurate grapevine.
- Common "CYA" behaviours; too many CC and BCC emails
- Red tape and over-elaborate approval processes.
- Hidden agendas and Turf wars.
- Energy draining and joyless interactions and too many meetings.
- High staff turnover.
- A high fear factor among employees.

It has been apparent for some time that both our political and commercial leaders are in a state of change and want and need help to reinstate trust and integrity. But is this really possible? We are bombarded everyday with fresh stories which question these same leaders' honesty and behaviour. Can they really claw back the ground they've lost and regain our trust?

I believe the answer is a BIG yes!

## High And Low Trust Organisations

When I work with companies on how to gain and maintain trust, I reference Stephen M R Covey's 'Speed of Trust' research explaining trust as a business driver. He notes that when people trust you in business, they trust both your character and your competence.

To quote Covey: "Think about it this way: When trust is low, in a company or in a relationship, it places a hidden "tax" on every transaction: every communication, every interaction, every strategy, every decision is taxed, bringing speed down and sending costs up. My experience is that significant distrust doubles the cost of doing business and triples the time it takes to get things done. I also have found some leaders fail to realise is the power behind being perceived as having high integrity and being trustworthy. These perceptions truly do impact business results. Yet, often our behaviour as leaders drives just the opposite."

Trusted leaders get many rewards: engaged employees, retention of top talent, positive work culture, and—most importantly business results. Why is it that so few realise the power of integrity and trust as business tools?  As a leader, where do you stand?

## $23 Billion Deal Done With A Handshake?

Warren Buffett—CEO of Berkshire Hathaway the third wealthiest person in the world, is an example of both character and your competence.  For example, he completed a major acquisition of McLane Distribution (a $23 billion company) from Wal-Mart. As public companies, both Berkshire Hathaway and Wal-Mart are subject to all kinds of market and "Due Diligence". Typical merger of this size would take several months to complete and cost several million dollars to pay for accountants, auditors, and attorneys to verify and validate all kinds of information.

However, in this instance, because both parties operated with high trust, the deal was made with one two-hour meeting and a handshake.

## The Secret: High Trust, High Speed, Low Cost.

This is definitely true when people look to see whether a leader is trustworthy. They look first for character; does the leader have integrity; do they tell the truth and keep their word? Do they have good intentions; do they have the best interests of the enterprise at heart? Then they look for competence; does the leader have the capabilities necessary to do his or her job; does the leader get results?

When people see that a leader is trustworthy in these ways, and is also far-sighted, has a clear vision, is passionate, courageous, wise and generous, they'll fully align around that person. They'll commit to them as leader.

All the elements are important of course, but trustworthiness is the bottom line. Trust has emerged as a new line in the P & L of business; one to be developed and delivered. Watson Wyatt study showed that high trust companies outperform low trust companies by nearly 300%!

## Integrity And Its Relationship To Trust?

"You cannot talk your way out of situations you have behaved yourself into; you can however behave your way out of them faster than you think."

Coaching Leaders over the last three decades in how to gain

and maintain trust, can be difficult, but those who pay the price reap the long-term trust dividend.

Your job as a leader is to go first, to extend trust first. Not a blind trust without expectations and accountability, but rather a "smart trust" with clear expectations and strong accountability built into the process. The best leaders always lead out with a decided propensity to trust, as opposed to a propensity not to trust. As Craig Weatherup, former CEO of PepsiCo said, "Trust cannot become a performance multiplier unless the leader is prepared to go first."

As a leader, where do you stand? Here's your challenge:

1. Reflect and think about a person who had confidence in you and as a result extended to you their trust

2. Write a list of what that person did or said that inspired you

3. Plan to demonstrate these behaviours with everyone

Trust in organisational strategies and in top management is the most critical component in creating commitment, rather than just compliance, toward a common goal. Achieving that trust, however, can be difficult.

But now is the time for companies and CEOs to deliver long-term performance by communicating frequently and honestly, and by considering the role of business in society. Now is the time for business to prove its commitment to profit and purpose. Now is the time for business to become more trustworthy. And it starts with the leader.

## About Jim Hetherton

An international coach, consultant, keynote speaker, and trainer Jim has held leadership and management positions at Tesco, OnTrack International, he was principal consultant at Franklin Covey.

He has extensive experience in business management and learning and development at both strategic and operational levels.

His clients have been enriched with Jim's delivery style which is continually described by delegates as 'inspirational and life changing', he has helped many thousands of people to improve the way they work. He has worked with people at all levels from a wide range of organisations, including IBM, GE, Jaguar Cars, Barclays Bank, GSK, BP, Merrill Lynch HBOS, Hewlett Packard, RBS, Vodafone, Merck and other FTSE 100 companies.

Jim's goal is to leave you better than he found you. Contact him for a free consultation.

*https://www.linkedin.com/in/jim-hetherton-52030a2/*

# The Hidden Power Within

**Erik Dvergsnes**

The very last gift Steve Jobs gave to his close friends and family was at his own memorial. Steve gave everyone a book by Yogananda called *Autobiography of a Yogi*; a book about self-realization.

Why do you think Steve Jobs wanted his closest friends and family to be left with such a message and memory of him to learn about self-realization? Think about it. The very last message to leave to the people he liked and trusted most. The most important message he wanted to share with the world: *Learn how to be self-realized!*

How many people today, are really living and operating from their true potential and are self-realized? The same goes for companies. What companies are limitless and operate at their absolute best?

Right now, so many people are operating from and living in fear due to the pandemic. It's like they are caught in the headlights; they are so frightened or nervous that they don't know what to do.

Panicking and being nervous is not the case for people who are self-realized, and this is where I want you to start your journey towards and operate from.

In 2015, I was fortunate to be introduced to a global award-winning educational system led by Dr Tony Quinn which had a profound effect on me. I partook in the Educo seminar (*) and was introduced to my true self, the power within! It was a life changing experience, people attended from numerous countries and numerous backgrounds within the corporate arena and together we all shared one common purpose, the innate power inside ourselves!

It is the same power that automatically heals a wound when you cut yourself, it pumps your heart, circulates your blood and grows your fingernails. This is the power you can learn to connect to and call upon to support you. It has nothing to do with religion. For those who have reached this higher level, which by the way is easy to do and available for everyone, it is the path to self-realization, and this is the message that Steve Jobs wanted his family and friends to become aware of. It is an actual Power and the more this power can freely express itself the better it is for you, and for humanity.

As we grow up, we are influenced by our surroundings, parents, teachers, the news and all these impressions form programs that are stored in our sub, or, unconscious mind.

According to Sigmund Freud, human beings are operating from 6/7th's of our unconscious mind, "unconscious like being knocked out and no control" and only 1/7th of our conscious mind. Therefore, whatever you have consumed from external influences, including your own thoughts and your own internal dialogue become deeply imprinted programs in your mind and these programs control your life. Where you are in your life right now, is a result of your thinking! Have you heard the expression "Life follows thought!" These programs in your unconscious operate on autopilot and run your life. Some people have good programs and are generally in a good state, so obviously they have managed to give themselves the right mental programs, but the majority are struggling and don't know why.

The good news is that you can change this, and this is where the power comes in. The more you can manage to connect to and increase your power, also referred to as increasing your vibration, the more you can control your thoughts, and this will bring you closer to self-realization. How quickly depends on your ability to let go of limiting programs that block you from connecting to your true power.

For instance, you can communicate with your power and you can call up happiness and instantly you will feel happy and start laughing. You can call up energy and in seconds your body overflows with a surge of energy. You can even call up health and heal yourself and stop viruses and infections in your body.

For you to start this journey the key is to be able to control your thoughts and connect with real life. Most people today are trapped in thoughts and worries like; what if I get sick, what if my immune system is not strong, what if I lose my job? By adopting this way of thinking, they begin creating a movie in their head about the worst possible scenarios and if you keep running this movie repetitively it will become stored as a real experience in your mind and you can actually cause physical illness. Therefore, it is vital to learn to control your thoughts and the best way to start is to go outside in nature. Walk outside and use all your senses, immerse your whole body and mind connecting with nature so there is no room for thoughts. You have now switched into life and you are experiencing real life and not life seen through layers of thoughts. For the majority of time when people are out in nature they are consumed with their mobile phones and trapped in thoughts and never experience and connect with true life.

The second tip is to write down a list of all your happy memories from your childhood up to where you are now. Choose the ones that mean the most to you, write down a mini script where you re-live that memory and again use all your senses. By doing this you start re-imprinting your good and happy memories and instantly you will notice a positive shift in your state. Ask a family member or a friend to remind you of some great memories you have shared together, the key is to keep asking questions, so you go into such detail about your memory that they appear real again. By telling the story again you re-imprint your happy memories and you will completely change your state to feeling happy and great and through this approach you are strengthening your immune system. You can do this with your kids, family members and colleagues, and take turns to recount your best memories. In a company, you can encourage your staff to record a great memory to video and share it. Now you have loads of happy staff, the spirit of the company is lifted and as a bonus everyone gets to know each other more creating a stronger bond like a family.

Combining these simple but powerful tips will put you in a much better place to perform the best creative thinking. Now you can plan with a clear mind and a much happier state for what to do with the situation you are in. If you have too many thoughts consuming all your mind, there is no room for the power to express itself. If you look at your situation through thoughts of fear and worries it can ruin your life. So, take the time to go outside, embrace nature SO MUCH, that there is no room for thoughts, then be still and notice what comes up?

Now is the time to use creative thinking and plan the best way out of your situation.

The seminar I took part in taught me so much about myself including reaching self-realisation. I really hope the tips that I have shared can be of help to you right now.

When you are in control of this power you create magic on all levels. This can happen individually, between people, in a company and between countries. Two friends of mine Susan Morris and Josh Stewart who also partook in the Educo training have taken their learning of the model to an extraordinary level and I have included some snippets of their stories below.

Please connect with me on LinkedIn as I would love to hear how you are doing and if I can be of any help to you right now. I am also happy to share with you more insights from the seminar if that is of interest.

### Susan Morrice – founder and CEO of Belize Natural Energy (BNE)

"When I understood what my true capacity was, my innate gifts, I used the steps outlined on the Educo seminar and Mike

Usher, myself and a group beat all odds, go against what everyone said was impossible and discover the first oil in Belize. The Educo seminar uncovers the layers, including doubt and fear, letting our full capacity be all we were born to Be!

### Josh Stewart, founder and CEO of X-jet valued at €2Billion

On the Educo seminar Josh created the vision for his company X-jet and from the birth of the company to the summer of 2019 X-jet has become the number one in private jets in the Americas and in Europe. As Josh moved his operation to The United Arab Emirates (UAE), he set out to do more magic, leading the UAE and Belize to sign a bilateral economic cooperation agreement, all built on the same model coming out from attending the Educo seminar.

Please connect with me on LinkedIn as I would love to hear how you are doing and if I can be of any help to you right now.

## References

- The Educo Seminar https://www.educoworld.com/ - Tony Quinn, originator of The Educo® Model.

- Susan Morrice – founder and CEO of BNE, interviewed by Forbes magazine https://www.forbes.com/sites/rebeccaponton/2019/12/15/having-helped-discover-belizes-only-commercial-wells-susan-morrice-envisions-its-post-oil-future/#776f00ff28e8

- Josh Stewart, founder and CEO of X-jet, interviewed by Shane Cradock-http://shanecradock.com/business-2/highlights-interview-josh-stewart-ceo-x-jet/

- The UAE and Belize sign a bilateral economic cooperation agreement https://www.oilandgasmiddleeast.com/drilling-production/35312-uae-and-belize-sign-bilateral-economic-cooperation-agreement

## About Erik Dvergsnes

Erik Dvergsnes is an IT technology architect at Aker BP Norway with a special focus on the Oracle Cloud platform. Erik has always had an entrepreneurial spirit and passion for helping and supporting others. Working in a variety of business areas from the oil industry to Finance and telecommunications, Erik has been able to support his technical skills with real world  commercial experience in large organisations like Cap Gemini, Shell Oil, Predictive Communications, Deutsche Bank and BP Norway.

*LinkedIn: linkedin.com/in/erik-dvergsnes-2619213*

*Email: erikdvergsnes@gmail.com*

# Communicating In Times Of Crisis: The Impact Of Leadership Styles On Communication

## Sandi Goddard

It is a given that leadership, good or bad, impacts the bottom line. It will also influence the final outcome, of an organisation or a nation, in times of crisis. And today, more than at any time in recent history, the world needs great leaders.

But what defines a great leader? In her book, *Fast Track To The Top*, based on interviews with global business leaders, clinical psychologist, Professor Ros Taylor lists her *10 Commandments of Leadership* as indicative of great leadership skills.

They need to:

1. Problem Solve

2. Achieve Results

3. Have Drive

4. Have Interpersonal Skills

5. Trust

6. Manage Stress

7. Embrace Change

8. Be Self-Aware

9. Have Strong Negotiation Skills

10. Be Confident

Ref: Taylor, R. & Humphry, J. (2002). Fast Track to the Top. Kogan Page

Above all, in unprecedented circumstances, I would suggest that leaders need to:

- Have the vision and the foresight to plan strategically
- To act decisively
- And to communicate well and with compassion

Some of these skills have certainly been evident in our leaders since December 2019, when the world first became aware of the coronavirus.

But what about their leadership styles? How effective have they shown themselves to be?

## Leadership Styles

Leaders are only human. In the face of war, famine, economic downturn or a pandemic, they will naturally be concerned for themselves, their family, their friends, their business, their finances, their communities and governments. They need to be able to manage themselves in order to care for others.

And how they care for their people and lead them through a crisis will be reflected in whether they retain the loyalty of their teams and in consequence a viable enterprise.

This is true on a global scale. In times of uncertainty people demand strong leadership. If leaders are perceived as weak, dispassionate, harsh, the outcome could be dissension, unrest or even civil war.

The Chinese leadership take an Autocratic approach, effective in getting things done – for instance building a hospital in ten days.

But failure can be catastrophe. When the outbreak began, local officials, perhaps fearful of passing negative information up the ladder, tried to minimise the gravity of the situation. When Dr Li Wenliang an ophthalmologist at Wuhan Central Hospital messaged fellow doctors alerting them to a SARS-like virus beginning to effect patients, police visited him and ordered him to stop 'spreading rumours'.

Once they accepted there was a problem, the Chinese government reacted efficiently and effectively. But would the results have been different, would there have been so many deaths worldwide, if the relationship was more open and trusting?

At the other end of the scale, we have the UK Government exhibiting a Laissez Faire form of leadership. Boris Johnson appealed to the public, trusting us to use our good judgement, to be sensible, fair and disciplined. It became clear that restraints had to be imposed to save us from ourselves.

And then there is the Narcissistic style, arguably the approach taken by Donald Trump in the USA. For weeks, he played down the virus as 'flu and even when he bowed to the evidence and scientific advice, he seemed to place his reputation above the health of his nation.

Often risk takers, such leaders can be extraordinarily productive, carrying many before them with their rhetoric, but their lack of restraint and self-knowledge, their belief in their own gifts, infallibility, and enemies that block their way, can prove disastrous. Only time will tell, in this instance, how effective his style was in curtailing the damage of the pandemic in the United States.

The Governor of Ohio State, Mike DeWine, illustrated how effective an Authoritative approach can be. He put his people first. Despite being ridiculed for his actions, he installed protective measures before there was a single case of coronavirus in his State. Ultimately, his decisions may have saved hundreds, possibly thousands, of lives.

The Visionary style of leadership is probably best exemplified by Unilever's CEO, Alan Jape. On 13th March 2020, as soon as the WHO (World Health Organisation) confirmed a pandemic, Unilever immediately launched actions to protect their teams across the globe. This ranged from remote working to strict hygiene protocols and social distancing for laboratory and distribution centre staff.

Or by Marco Alvera CEO of Snam, Italy's natural gas infrastructure company, based in Lombardy. Italy was possibly the worst affected European nation and Lombardy, Italy's worst affected region. The lock down began on 9th March but prior to that Snam had already established remote working for 2300 of its 3000 employees.

The remainder had to continue undertaking maintenance work in the field so their leadership activated measures from clothing and shift patterns to special accommodation in order to protect them as well as they could.

Ref: Gale, A. (03.04.2020) What happens next: COVID-19 lessons from Italian CEOs. Management Today

For many SMEs, despite surviving economic troughs, a pandemic would be a new experience. Like Phill Allen, CEO of ALLPaQ Packaging, market leaders in the design and supply of bioprocess containers, they would have to take an Agile approach if they were to deal successfully with such an unprecedented crisis. Phill and his team had to learn quickly, and on a daily basis, focusing on Government sources to provide the up to date information they would need in order to plan, adapt and act.

## Communication

While nations and enterprises have taken varying approaches to dealing with the pandemic, what struck me, above all, was the significance of Communication skills. How well a government communicated information across all sectors, to the way a business leader disseminated this information to stakeholders.

Take the Chinese Government. Using their sophisticated communications' network they informed, tracked and controlled their people, taking stringent measures to lock down the epicentre. By April 7th 2020, approximately three and a half months from the start of the outbreak, the leadership could report no new deaths from the coronavirus.

To further illustrate the serious nature of the virus, on 10th February, President Xi Jinping took the unprecedented step of being televised visiting a Beijing hospital, donning a face mask and having his temperature checked.

Some incidents however, such as shaving the heads of nursing staff on camera to show their selfless devotion, seemed unnecessarily humiliating and dispassionate.

In the USA three leaders stood out:

- Dr. Anthony S. Fauci, Director of NIH's National Institute of Allergy and Infectious Diseases (NIAID) repeatedly emphasised the importance of articulating exactly what was known and still needed to be understood about the threat. He argued for science above rumour and pseudo-scientific theories and solutions. As the United States' leading expert on infectious diseases, he is widely respected for his ability to explain science. He repeatedly stepped up after the president during televised briefings to correct pronouncements such as the speed with which a vaccine would be available.

- Andrew Cuomo, Governor of New York State, held daily briefings from the state capital building or New York Convention Centre. He put forward the facts, followed by the challenges and would end with human interest stories. Although he was speaking to New York the whole country tuned in to what were labelled by The Washington Post "The Cuomo Monologues: part briefing, part sermon, part inspirational talk."

- Governor Mike DeWine of Ohio State, equally effective, had a different style. Calm and meticulous, he called upon his communications professionals, and his own 40 years of government experience, to communicate to Ohioans daily about this most dramatic upheaval in their lives. He calmly and simply explained the ongoing situation in his briefings, even spelling out each letter of the website, to be sure he was understood.

For global businesses, Unilever has epitomised the way many businesses communicated with stakeholders. From the first message on 13th March to alert all staff of the actions required to protect themselves from Covid-19, which clearly itemised what was expected from each department, there has been regular contact to ensure their people are kept well informed and in the loop.

Others communicated their Corporate Social Responsibility credentials. Coca-Cola redeployed their staff and manufacturing bases to make face shields. JCB redeployed to produce shields for Dyson's new ventilators. The list is endless.

The majority of businesses maintained strong communication links with customers. For example, Tesco's CEO Davis Lewis with his weekly customer information emails. While others continued to advertise. Many felt a 'sales message' inappropriate in such circumstances. Birds Eye communicated "reassurance", focusing on those moments of connection and mutual support that people were demonstrating during the crisis, adopting a sensitive, supportive stance.

Ref: Marketing Week 08:02 (08.04.2020)

SMEs comprise the majority of businesses worldwide. In the UK, ALLpaQ Packaging employs less than 20 personnel. At the beginning of 'lock down' in Great Britain, CEO Phill Allen spoke to his team daily providing factual, up-to-date information. When it became clear that theirs would be key-worker status he ensured that all possible protections where in place and that every individual understood the threats of continuing to work, allowing them to make that choice.

## Conclusion

I think the key take-aways in terms of communication are to:

Understand your audience. Be authentic. Have clarity of Message. Over invest - say more, say it clearly, say it honestly, and say it again and again.

The speed and spread of COVID-19 brought great leaders to the fore. But poor leaders beware. Your positions are not set in stone. If you did not give due care, consideration and compassion to your people then it will be no surprise if they show no loyalty or consideration for you, your business or political party.

Uncertain times make leaders of us all. They call upon us to Consider, Decide, Act, Communicate.

## About Sandi Goddard

Sandi Goddard FInstLM has a 35-year background in branding and marketing communications.

She is a business consultant whose focus is on expansion, dramatic growth and exit. Sandi is a Fellow of The Institute of Leadership & Management and member of the Association of Coaching

*sandi@goddard-delaney.com*

*+ 44 (0) 7710 115 332*

# Everybody Has A Plan
# Until They Get Punched In The Mouth
## (The Mike Tyson Effect)

**Gilles Rochefort**

Mike Tyson is not generally known for his philosophical insights. But this simple and visceral quote from his boxing past is an effective metaphor describing the impact of disruptions - especially big ones.

We have just received a collective 'punch in the mouth' from the pandemic. Clearly meaning that our plans are now in flux. So, how do we respond? If you're a manager of people, their coach, this article is about adjusting your approach to keep them engaged. If you're an individual contributor, pass it on to your boss if you think they might benefit.

### The Value Of Engagement

As the saying goes, "Top performers join good companies but leave them because of a bad boss".

Retention might not be the main issue today, but employee engagement and productivity are. And they depend on the relationship people have with their bosses. Managers that have positive relationships with their direct reports are more likely to have a motivated, productive, and loyal workforce.

Given these challenging times of managing from a distance, the risks of lower engagement and lower productivity are greater than usual. Managers that can figure out a way to continue developing (coach) their direct reports are more likely to ensure they are working at their highest level.

## Measuring The Relationship

Who knows how long 'working-from-home' will last. But one thing is likely. The relationship between managers and their direct reports will either get better or worse. They will not remain the same. The best way to determine where the individual relationship is now, where it's going, and how to make it more effective in these difficult times, is to measure it. Establish baseline metrics, formulate a development plan to be a better manager under the circumstances, and measure again when this ordeal is over. Only then can an objective and personalized appraisal of the relationship be made.

## Removing Barriers

Research - and common sense - has shown that the biggest challenge for managers in coaching their people is finding time to do it. Provided they know how. Under the new 'work-from-home' circumstances, managers now have more time to conduct one-on-one coaching. An exceptional opportunity not to be missed.

The key is preparation. Managers need to take the time and make the effort to fully prepare for each meeting – individual or group. Also allow the direct reports to prepare in advance by agreeing and setting goals for each meeting and sending an agenda for each meeting. Have questions ready. Offer to be the note taker. Send notes for confirmation of meeting content and summary of next steps. Finally, every meeting should include a discussion on the status of individual situations and how the manager can help.

## Showing You Care

To paraphrase Sun Tzu, 'When you are far way, pretend to be near.' He said it as a war tactic to deceive enemies, but the same tactic is very effective in coaching direct reports who work at a distance in normal times. It's especially true today with social distancing and everyone is far away. The attribute with the strongest correlation with coaching competency is the amount of 'Individual Attention' given by managers to their direct reports. In other words, showing them, that they care. These days, the best way to do that is for managers to meet them virtually, often, and one at a time.

## Being Credible

No matter the frequency or deftness to communicate, if managers are not respected or at least not fully, their message will fall on deaf ears. Especially new and unproven managers. All the skills in the world will not change the outcome.

If credibility is an issue, and the manager is aware, then selecting someone from the team of direct reports who already has the respect of their peers – a 'captain' of sorts - could be delegated the assignment of passing on 'coaching' messages that the new manager is unable to. Getting the support of one internal and respected 'leader' might be less challenging than trying to win over an entire team.

## Demonstrating Desire

Managers who are respected and sincerely care about their people must also demonstrate it - with actions that match their intentions. For example, setting up a virtual meeting with a direct report and not use the 'Video' option is almost like telling them 'my door is always open' but in fact it's not. So, managers must show their face and make the chat more personal - P2P (person to person).

Being flexible will also serve the manager well. Allowing direct reports more latitude, new freedoms, or greater responsibility in some situations will demonstrate their desire to make them better. There is an old saying, "if you want someone to be responsible, give them responsibilities". Seems simple to do but unless managers are prepared to be flexible, it's not. Many managers find it extremely hard to give up control.

## Being Interested

Empathy can only happen if a manager knows what the other person is thinking and feeling. And that happens when managers ask. So, they should stop trying to be interesting and instead be better prepared to ask questions and listen with interest. If a reaction by the managers is appropriate, they should make it, and then invite a response.

Everyone's experience with these new circumstances are likely different. Some direct reports are surrounded with loved ones. Others are alone. Some are working in cramped quarters. Others are in comfortable home offices. Some are constantly distracted by their environment. Others are looking for distractions to keep their minds active. The stress levels will vary with individual circumstances. So, managers should be actively listening to get a clearer understanding of the situation and show - not just say - they get it.

## The New Normal

Working from home because of the pandemic may not be the last punch we will take. The best laid plans are subject to change again. But regardless of the new changes, one objective for people managers should remain constant – continue to effectively coach their people.

In summary, effective coaching is the best approach to keeping people engaged and to sustain productivity until the pandemic is over. As a people manager it begins with respect and ends with competence. So, they need to check their level of credibility, manage their time wisely, show they care, and personalize their interactions. Ask, listen, and respond in kind.

In the face of big disruptions and changing plans, from Mike Tyson to John Geenleaf Whittier, the following is a great reminder to rest, get up, and keep going.

### Don't Quit

John Greenleaf Whittier

When things go wrong as they sometimes will,

When the road you're trudging seems all up hill,

When the funds are low and the debts are high

And you want to smile, but you have to sigh,

When care is pressing you down a bit,

Rest if you must, but don't you quit.

Life is strange with its twists and turns

As every one of us sometimes learns

And many a failure comes about

When he might have won had he stuck it out;

Don't give up though the pace seems slow—

You may succeed with another blow.

Success is failure turned inside out—

The silver tint of the clouds of doubt,

And you never can tell just how close you are,

It may be near when it seems so far;

So stick to the fight when you're hardest hit—

It's when things seem worst that you must not quit.

Ref http://www.yourdailypoem.com/listpoem.jsp?poem_id=1820

## About Gilles R. Rochefort

Gilles discovered early in his career that 'managing the people part' is often the most difficult and most important aspect of any organization.

He went on to empirically research the value of management coaching and how it might be more accurately defined, measured, and applied. His research led him to successfully test his coaching methodology (PMC) with several international firms.

He published *'Tales from the Playing Field - a new strategy for Business Management Coaching'* (Woodley & Watts, 2000) and launched Personalized Management Coaching (PMC). He has since licensed the rights to the model and assessments to other consultants.

Today, the PMC program supports consultants in the Americas, the United Kingdom, Europe, Middle East, and Asia. It continues to deliver on its promise of improving engagement, retention, development, and succession.

New technologies and management disruptions have led to his contribution to *'Digital Coach – In the Era of Artificial Intelligence'* (Amazon.com, 2019).

Preferred Contact links are:

*www.pmcoaching.com*

*pmcoaching@rogers.com*

*LinkedIn: Gilles R. Rochefort*

*Personalized Management Coaching*

# Lessons From Desert Island Survival!
## Leadership In Business During The Pandemic Crisis

### Steven Shove MBA, DipM

*If people are able to survive and thrive in the wild with few or apparently no resources, against all the odds and in the harshest of environments, they can certainly survive and thrive in business, at school and in their personal and family lives too.*

If ever these words were needed, it is now! You have the means to see this crisis through!

### Introduction – Marooned On A Deserted Island

Many businesses have seen between 75% and 100% of their business revenues dry up almost overnight, especially if they are related to industries such and leisure, tourism and retail. Within my own circle of friends, family and associates, I've seen a software company that serves the hair and beauty industry suffer from more than half its salons stopping standing orders and direct debits. Another organisation that runs clubs for children had all its activities shut down with immediate effect and my own companies that serve the schools, business and leisure markets have experienced a similar downturn in demand. These are examples of organisations that are the primary casualties of this current crisis.

Secondary casualties include a marketing company that

serves the retail sector and two rental companies that have seen their tenants unable to pay.

At the time of writing, Debenhams and Cath Kidston have just called in the administrators and untold suppliers and creditors face never being paid. Airlines are grounded and for many, help is not on its way.

In this chapter, I equate what is happening to us economically during the pandemic crisis with what happens when people find themselves suddenly marooned and most likely injured on a deserted tropical island. There is no immediate escape. You just have to survive and do what you can!

I know this situation well as I teach survival skills on such islands and then draw parallels from lessons learned to peoples' businesses and personal lives too.

In this current crisis there is another complication too. An impending tsunami of untold economic damage that is surely on its way. As it gathers pace and volume and roars towards our shores, its effects on businesses and people's lives will be incredible. Potential total devastation for many, but a new landscape of opportunity.

## Survival Priorities And A Moment For Absolute Clarity – Cash Is King!

Whenever anyone is washed up on a desert island or finds themselves lost or injured in the wild, there is one single thing that should be on that person's mind – SURVIVAL!

People often believe that water and food are the top survival priorities and focus all their efforts erroneously on these. In the first minutes or hours of survival, these are often lower down on the list of priorities than one might think.

You can survive three minutes without air, a similar time if bleeding very heavily, three days without water, three weeks without food and broadly three months without company before you start to lose your marbles through lack of social interaction. This is called the rule of 3's and informs the survivor with absolute clarity of their survival priorities.

There is one other priority too that quickly makes all the difference. That of shelter and as with shelter people feel more secure and have the opportunity to think and take stock. They will generally become extremely innovative and make better decisions.

In business terms, these priorities translate into cash flow and cash reserves. Immediate risks are mitigated and the temporary financial shelter this brings provides time for you to think. Cash is king!

Once cash flow and reserves are secured in the immediate and nearer term, leaders can find the breathing room to think about their medium and longer-term objectives. Where they choose to focus and when will make all the difference!

The following diagram shows when and where efforts should be targeted.

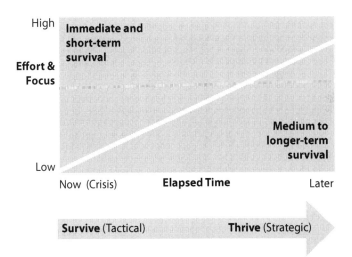

*Really Wild Method – © Copyright 2020 Steven Shove*

If the beginning of the crisis is now and your business is in trouble, then your actions need to be very tactical and focused indeed, on efforts to secure your business's immediate survival. This is not always appreciated, as some people choose to keep their heads in the sand about what is now upon them. They may even have notions of timely rescue which they should certainly not rely upon.

As your situation improves or if your business is thriving because of the pandemic, then your efforts can be directed further towards the more strategic end of the spectrum.

When a tsunami forms it drains all of the water away from the beaches and out to sea. In such moments, all the rocks and debris on the sea floor become exposed to view.

For businesses that have seen demand collapse and bills go unpaid, the equivalent of the outward tide is their cash disappearing, and just like the rocks and debris, all their dangerous costs and overheads become vividly clear.

If your business in trouble, urgently take a good look at your financial position and act immediately to remove the rocks and debris that you feel you need to without delay:

1. Cut all unnecessary/unaffordable expenses

2. Delay existing financial commitments as fast and for as long as you can

3. Collect any unpaid revenues

4. Bill whomever you are able to and seek early payment

5. Re-negotiate to a quid pro quo exchange of services where you can

6. Apply for any grants, credit lines or government aid as appropriate

Remember, your priority right now is to keep your business alive just long enough to come up with and execute a better medium to longer term plan.

Cutting costs is not always easy, especially if it effects a valued supplier or member of your team. Where you need to cut costs, cut them, but do so in a manner that safeguards those relationships as best you can. Another option is to delay them.

With regards to spend on strategic projects, if you are facing a financial crisis, you will need to cut or suspend costs here too. Don't let vanity or the love of a pet project prevent you from doing so.

Once you have executed all the above, only then have you created time to think about developing and executing a more sustainable plan to ensure your continued survival over the medium and longer term.

By sustainable, I mean a plan to generate renewed and ongoing revenue streams with net inflows of cash to your business.

### Time To Lead!

You are not out of danger yet, just secure for a while until different and potentially even greater challenges arise, so priorities still need to be managed. Expect that your circumstances will continue to change and again, do not rely on being rescued!

It is now time to lead through:

1. Clear thinking and direction - rallying your team
2. Taking stock and gathering resources
3. Innovation and creativity
4. Collaboration and great teamwork
5. Continued timely action

## Clear Thinking And Direction – Rallying Your Team

A famous Victorian explorer once advised adventurers in his handbook to stop and enjoy a smoke of their finest tobacco should they ever become lost. The reasons, to calm the nerves and allow the mind to rest which would then allow them to either retrace their steps or set a plan in place towards safety.

In today's crisis, we are not in a position to retrace steps, so a plan towards safety and beyond is the only course to take.

As a leader, take time for calm reflection in any manner you can, then rally your team with your vision and plans to give them reassurances that you will prevail.

When rallying your team, be candid about your situation. This will build valuable trust, and everyone will know where they stand.

The plan I shared with my team was as follows. It was preceded by full disclosure of our financial position along with the date, that without the plan, we would run out of cash.

My initial plan and vision were as follows:

1. To maximise immediate cash flow and reserves

2. To leverage "whatever resources" we have available in new and creative ways

3. To focus on what our customers most need today and to think differently about how we can help them now. It is probable that needs will have changed!

4. To come together with an incredible sense of urgency, focus and flexibility

5. To serve and help others along the way in any way we can. As a society, we have a great responsibility to help regardless of financial gain

As I shared my vision of the future, I also painted a picture of how three of our most common business challenges might also be solved during this time of crisis – limited access to land, limited availability of requisite skills, and the demand by many of our clients to want our services, all too frequently, at the same time.

I asked for their input and ideas and concluded the meeting with immediate actions and a schedule to regroup on a frequent and regular basis.

## Taking Stock And Gathering Resources

When stranded on a desert island there is an abundance of resources that can help your situation, from man made flotsam found on the beach to natural resources at the jungle's edge. With these you can source or purify water, collect, catch, hunt or trap food, build shelter, navigate, administer first aid and all manner of other things. In order to achieve these though, you must first take stock of what you have, scour your surroundings for whatever else might be available and then get creative with what you can do with it all. It's an exciting phase and one I have enjoyed first-hand.

With the right attitude, creativity and determination you can quickly move from a position of just getting by to one of real comfort and wellbeing – from surviving to thriving!

In business, the resources to look out for and examine for their possibilities include:

- People and relationships
- Physical assets such as land, buildings, tools and materials
- Financial assets or sources
- Intangible assets such as intellectual property, skills or know how
- The services you offer

In a crisis, each must be examined through a lens of discerning optimism and critical decisiveness!

Their qualities and uses, value or otherwise may have become or have the potential to become very different from the norm. Consider their qualities as though searching for and examining materials whilst surviving on a desert island and ask the following questions:

- **People and relationships** – are they reliable, inventive, disciplined, flexible, supportive, talented and more or less valuable today? Are there people now available to you that otherwise might not have been? Where are they and how could you use them?

- **Physical assets** such as land, buildings, tools, systems and materials – Do they remain assets or have they become liabilities. Are they generating positive or negative cash flow? Can they be re-purposed, disposed of or are they reliable just as they are for example? Is their value more or less than before?

- **Financial assets or sources** - how long will they last, have they been exhausted, are there more sources from which they can be derived, might you be able to put them to better use and make them more valuable than before?

- **Intangible assets** such as intellectual property, skills or know how – what exists and how is it delivered? In what format is it held and is this still fit for purpose? What can be created or repurposed in some way? Which new channels might it be distributed through and how? When all is said in done do these assets have the potential to be more valuable today than they were previously?

- **The services you offer** and have offered in the past, to whom and to what benefit? Have customer or market needs changed and if so, are your services now of higher or lower value to them? Can your existing products even be sold at the moment or do you have the resources available to create and distribute new ones of more immediate value?

I ran through these questions with my team and asked them to take them away and to discuss them with their families. I also asked them to write down all of their own talents, hobbies, skills and experiences. I wanted to see fully what resources we might have at our disposal, and I wanted a few more ideas too about which directions we could take. The results that came back were wonderfully positive.

In addition to the assets and capabilities I knew we had already, I was pleasantly surprised by the following. We also had:

- Access to various professionals who would otherwise not be available or affordable to us

- Creative skills in design, film making and IT at our disposal, some within the team and some outside it

- Customers who were willing to help us out if we helped them, and

- People still interested in our original vision and purpose

Ideas were shared and I had a host of information and a lot more resources to work with.

We had taken stock and gathered new resources. It was now time to get creative and use them.

Take stock in your business and see what resources and ideas you and your team can come up with!

## Innovate And Adapt – The Power Of Creativity And Making For Higher Ground

As I have demonstrated, even when stranded on a desert island, great things can be achieved. Once resources are gathered and creatively deployed, people can not only avoid immediate dangers, but they can also travel inland and to the safety of higher ground where they will enjoy even greater levels of security. With further creativity and adaptation, they can move quickly to a position of relative comfort. Should a tsunami arrive they need no longer worry. They can look forward with confidence to taking advantage of the new resources it will bring and to a new landscape of opportunity that will have changed beyond recognition.

Having cut costs, controlled short term reserves and cash flow, taken stock of all possible resources and begun to get the creative juices flowing, a business really only has four possible options to replace or grow its revenues. This is how a business will move to that higher ground and to a position of more robust safety and relative comfort. Your options are set out in the diagram below, a version of that created by the strategist Igor Ansoff in 1957.

1. To continue to sell existing products to existing customers or markets

2. To sell existing products to new customers or markets

3. To create new products and sell them into existing customers or markets

4. To create new products and sell them to new customers or markets

During the pandemic crisis, many companies are faced with the unique and frightening fact that their current market for their existing products has closed overnight. A market penetration strategy is therefore no longer viable. These companies will need to innovate and adapt to their new situation quicker than most.

**For those who have seen their face to face business opportunities close down**, the options to deliver value to existing customers are:

- To deliver value remotely, for example digitally or online, in printed form or via a delivery service. By asking existing customers what they need most now you may find that you can serve them even better by adapting your services or creating entirely new ones through a strategy of **product development.**

- Delivering existing face to face products to new markets might become an option through a strategy of **market development** but this is highly unlikely to be the case for the foreseeable future due to the pandemic. Planning for this, for after the crisis may be useful provided it doesn't distract you from the priority of surviving right now.

- Creating new products or services for new markets is definite-ly an option. Whilst this is normally considered to be the most difficult and risky of strategies, it may simply be a case of needs must. With your having taken stock of the resources you have to hand and with a creative hat on, the horizons and opportunities that open up by following a **diversification strategy** could be unlimited. It may be time to reset and reinvent your business from scratch!

**For those of you who have seen existing customer demand for your remotely delivered services close down,** the opportunities to sell them to new customer types or markets seems the logical option through a **market development strategy.** Could for example a leadership coach who has focused on the leisure industry now offer his or her services to the NHS or a company whose services are in unprecedented demand? Could a software service designed for a face to face audience be valuable to an online one?

**For those of you where demand for your business is now at a record high**, the danger is to miss the opportunities that surfing this wave might bring. In a cash rich situation and in circumstances that means even more resources and talent are available to you, perhaps it is time to gain a foothold in new markets by following a **market development strategy** into new geographies or sectors for example.

With such an abundance of resources at your disposal, the issues of time scarcity and access to talent can be more readily be overcome. Now may be just the time to open up new markets with newly invented products by following a strategy of **diversification.**

In the last two weeks, I have spoken with leaders of businesses that between them have pursued each and every one of these strategies. Their situations and circumstances are all very different and quite rightly, so are the paths they have taken.

To further inspire your thinking, here are a few things that I have observed some companies already do:

- When pubs and restaurants have closed, they have turned to delivery services

- When gyms, dance clubs and karate clubs for example have closed, they have developed online training courses and live streams of their sessions

- When schools have closed, they have delivered classes remotely

- As consulting and coaching firms have not been allowed to enter premises, their teams have remotely connected to engage

- One company, in finding a solution to delivering its services remotely, then set up a partnership to offer the same service to companies that faced the same challenges as it did. An entirely new business created overnight!

- During the 2008/9 crash my customer-base of top-tier blue chip companies collapsed overnight. Within a week I had my team selling a cut down version of our products to the mid-market sector. Whilst sales fell, we still succeeded to thrive another day, and found a whole new customer base in the process.

## Collaboration, Teamwork And Timely Action

Surviving on your own in the wild is much more difficult than surviving with others. Ideas are formed, shared, modified and made more brilliant. Workloads are distributed and progress made more quickly, the sick are cared for, defenses strengthened, morale boosted, and the chances for success and rescue increased.

In a crisis there is little time to dither. Stem the flow of cash leaving your business and safeguard reserves, take stock of your resources and decide who you want on your team, innovate, create and adapt and get moving to the high ground where there is comfort and security, and into the wave that will bring with it a world of opportunity.

## So, What Of My Businesses, You May Ask?

In my own and my team's quest to survive and thrive during this crisis, we have come together and secured the support of others to do the following.

Most of what we traditionally do is delivered in person, from within the boardroom or classroom to the forests, Arctic environments, jungles and mountains of the world. We are bringing the business and life lessons, and personal development support that we normally deliver outdoors, indoors, and making it available on demand so people can be supported wherever and whenever they need us!

Specifically, we have brought forward our plans to test market and deliver the following:

1. An on demand digital service for parents and schools who face the challenge of supporting their children's mental wellbeing and behaviours whilst facing lock down at home – not focused on the academic side of things though supportive of it, but focused specifically on the mental and wellbeing challenges that are being felt so very acutely at this time. We have some of the world's best explorers sharing their challenges and life lessons from their Antarctic, Arctic, jungle and desert expeditions for

example, alongside approaches from our proven methodology for success, the Really Wild Method®.

2. For companies and organisations, we are offering similar on demand services to help staff faced with the considerable personal and business challenges, stresses and anxiety caused by this crisis via on demand digital services and remote 1:1 coaching and mentoring support!

3. For investors interested in our traditional education business, an opportunity to invest early in an exciting project to establish a physical school and learning environment whilst the team have extra time to work on it.

4. For those itching to bring their families or teams together as soon as they are able, we are offering exclusive corporate and private events, trips and expeditions to those who love what we do – teaching people how to survive and thrive in the wild, to enjoy adventure and then apply those experiences and lessons to their lives back at home, in work and at school. We have made gift vouchers and pre-paid bookings available for purchase right away!

The team is also offering free live stream videos and has created various online communities for certain of our audiences, for our clients and others to use at this time.

## Conclusion

In times of crisis people achieve incredible things! I wish you every success and above all, that you and your families stay safe and well.

If I or my team can help in any way, you know where to find me.

## References

- Ansoff, Igor: Strategies for Diversification, Harvard Business Review, Vol. 35 Issue 5, Sep-Oct 1957, pp. 113-124

- Kephart Horace (1862-1931): Camping and Woodcraft, The University of Tennessee Press, 1988

## About Steven Shove MBA, DipM

Steven is an experienced business leader and performance coach, a respected thought leader and one of the UK's most highly qualified survival instructors who passionately applies the principles of "original human success" to businesses, teams and individuals seeking to thrive in today's ever demanding and increasingly competitive environments.

For nearly 30 years, Steven consulted to and successfully led a variety of international teams and businesses, improving performance across the myriad of business functions and industries but specialising in leadership, sales, business strategy and personal development.

Steven is the Founding Director of the Really Wild Group that offers performance improvement coaching and consulting services, educational events, executive retreats, camps and expeditions to the business, education and leisure sectors.

Steven and his teams deploy a powerful and proven methodology for success called the Really Wild Method® that uniquely equips and enables individuals and organisations to deliver superior performance with far greater consistency and predictability - in the most exciting, engaging and memorable of ways. The Really Wild Method® helps people thrive at every stage in life.

Today, Steven works with clients in the boardroom or classroom to remote places such as the Arctic and the jungles of the Amazon and Borneo.

*LinkedIn: www.linkedin.com/in/stevenshove*

# Authority Only Goes So Far

## Jo Baldwin Trott

It is the time to finally and completely reset our mindset on women, men and leadership. And to do that we need to get real. There are many challenging conversations going on right now due to the pandemic. I am presenting a solution as well as highlighting an issue. I am igniting an opportunity for change.

I have studied leadership since day 1. An authoritative and dictatorial parent created a platform for me to mull. Over why, how and what the outcome of a leadership style is. Thanks to this intensive and impactive training, naturally stemming from that parent's own parental training, my norm was presented to me. I soaked it up as a child and I stuck with it as an adult.

After travelling around Australia and attending university, in April 1997 my norm eventually drove me all the way to National Police Training College in Bramshill. I became a police officer, at last. This had always been my goal, my 'when I grow up' statement. I was thrilled to finally begin my journey and looked forward to 30 long years ahead.

What in fact, I had become, was authoritative myself. Naturally. Over the last decade in mentoring and supporting and guiding leaders in overcoming their difficulties in showing up, I know that I am not alone in pursuing a damaging career. A career that manifests our difficult childhood as an adult. An environment that presents the same scenarios and relationships we are familiar with, even if they were toxic.

After an enriching experience of training, of soaking up everything thrown at me, of rubbing shoulders with the big brass at Bramshill, I excitedly and thankfully drove one last time west on the M Bore, I mean 4. I couldn't wait to get on with it, to get out there and to make a difference.

I remember, clear as day, Day 1 on my new uniform group. Ten of us in the team. Lead by a witty and dedicated sergeant. I felt a big buzz in the room. Yes, I was the only woman in the group, but part of my training had been with this gender ratio, it was nothing new and that had been a nurturing, and collaborative experience. I assumed I was in for more of the same. That wasn't the case.

Looking back, I can now recognise that something was off. That the energy in the room was just a bit edgy as well as buzzy. Laughter, smiles, banter, usual copper stuff, but something was amiss. But I was the newbie, I was in my dream job and I ignored my gut and threw myself into learning and becoming part of a team.

What ensued for the next two and half years was disgraceful. For the purposes of this chapter I will focus on my role and actions and those of my leader, and his leader, and his leader's leader. This is a leadership book after all and the details of my sexual harassment matter on a deeper level but for a different conversation. However, the management of the situation does matter. And over time it destroyed my faith of the establishment. The very thing that we, as police officers were expected to be able to produce on tap to the outside World was missing on the inside, compassion. There was lots of brushing under the carpet, 'it could be worse' assurances and I learnt that the necessity for simply focussing on the job in hand was all that mattered. Something was done, but nowhere near enough and it was devastating to me so early on in my service.

I do not believe that the inaction was because of gender. As I changed jobs within the job I came across different levels of empathy and compassion from my managers, and obviously women managers, too. It was simply the system and blueprint for addressing such cases was not fully established like it is now. And that my managers simply didn't understand, sympathise let alone empathise. Compassion was saved for the public not dished out to the officers. Things had begun to change within the police back then but at that time the new processes for internal harassment and unfair treatment were in the distant future. And this wasn't the only time I came up against a situation of unfairness which was sidelined.

But for me, at that time, it was a big blow. The lack of justice for the person who behaved so badly enraged me but it was the lack of concern from my manager that gave me a feeling of worthlessness.

The obscure and sometimes perverse sense of humour used by the police to cope with awful situations, I adjusted to. The lack of consideration for our human-ness I didn't. And when I finally had the courage to leave and pursue teaching, I was hit full force by how I'd turned that part of me off.

How I had literally felt just a number.

## Reactionary Leadership And How It Fails

Policing is one of the toughest jobs on the planet. You are expected to pivot in a heartbeat from sympathetic bearer of bad news to proactive crowd controller of a violent group. The continuous adrenalin spikes and lulls: one minute a burglary in progress, the next an elderly confused lady in her nightdress. This relentless high and low state has, no doubt, a part to play in stress and ill health. Add shift work and often a less than ideal diet into the mix and you have a recipe for sickness. The life expectancy of a police officer after retirement is incredibly low.

The job of policing, particularly in a deprived, poor area, is to manage the saddest and worst of scenarios. Over the next few years and whilst in uniform I had ticked most of the boxes of dealing with the extremities in humanity.

I'd attended the dirtiest imaginable homes full of children, dogs, dog faeces and drug paraphernalia. I'd felt the brush of instant death from a stolen car moving at 50 miles an hour. I'd seen my life flash before me and fall into the Avon Gorge. And movie-worthy, I saw myself being blown up in an explosion when a woman with mental health issues produced a lighter from her dressing gown pocket. After she had filled her house with gas. It was a fast forward moment as me and a colleague whipped her out of her home. Ethan Hunt would have been proud.

But on the plus side my initiative for rebuilding the relations of youth within a community paid off. My evidence and court training paid dividends in my own family court case. And I obviously didn't get dragged off the bridge after all. I have learnt a level of resilience and I am able to talk to anyone and deal with any emergency that lands on my lap. Being a mum of two, there have been a few. I also got to chase Banksy and see his original works on the buildings of Bristol. I always liked them, wish I'd taken pictures.

A lot happened in my nine years of police service. A lot was expected of all of us, all the time. The requirements of the job on the streets was half what I expected. But the lack of compassion for doing the job and dealing with what we had to was a shock. We dealt with the crises, we arrested the right people, we dealt with the moment but then you just went home. The most sickening experience for me, interviewing a paedophile, the most distressing the road traffic accident of two elderly people. When it came to dealing with the disasters the leadership were second to none. But when it came to us and our feelings, they were a long way off the mark.

Reactionary leadership works on a level in any organisation. For us it cleared the screen of calls received and ticked the Home Office boxes to some extent. But it didn't do the very thing that should have been at the top of the priority list.

Look after the workers first.

The purpose for highlighting the incidents above is to

evidence that leadership in policing is management of one disaster after another. It is simply put, reactionary leadership. In policing there is a continuous stream of life or death situations. Of damage limitation and of conflict management that has arisen from an unforeseen event. This is what we are facing now. The pandemic has been a shock to all. It is like we have been given a pin-popped hand grenade. And that we are attempting to manage where it gets thrown. It is devastating and desperate to experience and on a level it requires a style of leadership just like policing.

## Leading With A Generosity To The Future

Public health and environment needs to be managed. Personnel too. But to manage this current situation without compassion is to pretend we're not human and not impacted by the pandemic on a deeper level. It is imagining that there won't be long-lasting impacts on our social structures and our industries, our education and our families. And, of course, our health care system. When we tune into compassion we contemplate what is to come.

With compassion we consider how the children missing their exams will cope with their careers. How will people behave when we can socialise again, will they want to? Will the children who are being trained to stay two metres away need support to become physically accepting once more.

By discounting the needs of self-employed mums; by disregarding the emotional drain of dealing with traumatic scenes in our hospitals and by underestimating the loneliness felt my millions of elderly people we are forgetting the bigger picture. We are neglecting our communities, our people. And that is preventable.

In some ways it's a wheat and chaff moment. The leaders who care are showing up. The leaders who pretend are not. We can see it on our phones, we can feel it in our hearts, and we are registering the genuine concern, the real sincerity and the warmth.

We have already seen the leaders who are turning the humanity tap off. The empty statements of promise and blanket reference. We have heard the voices who, try as they might, can not truly connect with us with empathy, possibly because they have never suffered or because they do not allow their true human-ness to shine through. This doesn't work in policing and it won't work now. We are all in need of genuine connection and simply being told what to do is not so easy to accept unless it is supported by consideration and support for the impact these choices are having.

Yes, reactionary leadership will get us through this situation, but ignoring the basic needs of how we feel will be disastrous too. It is the time for compassionate leading. So many are going through hell.

Compassion and collaboration can change our now, not statistics. Equality can change today not lip service. We are in remarkable times and a time when leaders of compassion and calm can shine their light the brightest. Currently some remarkable women are trending on social media as being the voices we want to listen to: Dr Jennie Harris and Angela Merkel to name but two.

## Our New Norm

To grow from this situation and create a new norm we need equality across the board. This can't wait, we can't ponder it is now that women need to lead, too. The drum has been banged enough, there are no excuses, the time is now.

There are many reasons why equality will create a brighter future, the most obvious being as Mary Page the Liberal Democrat Mayoral candidate stated, 'We must be sat at the table, not just be the meal'. How can a male dominated or solely male committee discuss with complete compassion and empathy: the needs of single mothers; the challenges faced by our nurses, 80% of which are female?

In the UK, if we continue at the same rate of growth, an equal gender 50:50 ratio in Parliament will be achieved in 50 years time. Drumming fingers for 2070 is unacceptable and inexcusable. Women leaders must step up and be supported now.

The 5050 Parliament organisation is doing this with great success through their *#AskHerToStand* and *#SignUpToStand* campaigns. But this model should be across every board in the land.

Generally women find it easier to demonstrate compassion. Most women missed out on the diploma on emotional camouflage. By and large women avoided the call and 'need to be strong'. Females are designed to ultimately care more openly and care most for each other. It's what we have evolved as and from. Evolution has created us such, that the man's job to hunt and to focus on solving the issue.

If we start now to balance the board tables, and value our accumulative strengths we can create new compassionate leadership teams. We can diffuse our unique complexities in gender and create supportive leadership teams.

We will emerge from our homes and our hospitals with a focus on compassion and community. We will evolve into much better states.

The lowest point as my time in policing was on the large council estate in my patch. For the third time in the same number of weeks I arrested the same youth. He'd only just come out of 'inside'. At 14 years young, he'd nicked another car and so I asked him the big question, 'Why, Carl*, why do it again?' His response stunned me, 'For the grub, Jo, I'm starving'. He explained more, 'Ma doesn't buy us any food n'or give us no money. At least inside I'll get some proper nosh'.

In that moment I felt true despair and frustration. I also had complete clarity. For our societies to change our choices need to change and our leadership style needs to change first.

In the meantime, I am dusting off my police hat as they're calling in retired officers. I may be back in uniform once more.

## About Jo Baldwin Trott

Jo Baldwin Trott helps influential leaders to leverage their brand by aligning their energy.

Jo has mentored Harley Street doctors, TV celebrities and even pop stars. Anyone who needs to show up and influence.

She is an International best selling author and is a lecturer for the London College of Style. Her next book, 'Women Leading' will be published in May 2020.

Jo is also a member of the Professional Speakers Association and a director for parliamentary equality group, 5050 Parliament.

Jo is based in London, loves California and writing songs.

Join Jo's conversation on LinkedIn *www.linkedin.com/in/jobaldwintrott,* check out her personal brand interviews on YouTube *https://youtu.be/h5X5XNmfSMw* or go to her website at *www.jobaldwintrott.com*

Call, email, Follow or Google Jo at:

*jo@jobaldwintrott.com*

*@jobaldwintrott*

# TRUE Leadership In A Crisis

## Nigel Allfrey and Mike Davis-Marks

### 'All Eyes Are On You'

The world is currently experiencing a crisis on an unprecedented level that hasn't been seen since the Second World War. A highly contagious virus, with no known treatments or vaccines has, in a matter of a few months become a global pandemic, which is infecting millions and killing thousands. Without being too melodramatic, the world finds itself again at war, this time against an invisible killer and humanity is for once, all on the same side.

The time for good leadership at international, national, local and within organisations and communities has never been greater and whilst leadership is often one of those skills that comes to the fore in a crisis, the ability to lead most effectively during a crisis should have been learned and honed long before the crisis arrives.

### Leadership Vs Management

But first things first. It is quite common for leadership and management to be considered one and the same thing, but they are not. A manager organises, but a leader inspires. A manager sets targets, but a leader sets a vision that everyone aspires to achieve. It is entirely possible (and sadly quite common) to be a good leader and a bad manager or a good manager and a bad leader, but at least a good leader realises his or her limitations as a manager and then develops and delegates to others to deliver the organisational skills. A bad leader doesn't.

We call the good leader a TRUE leader and a bad leader either a Passive or False leader and the good news is that everyone can learn to be a TRUE leader in time.

In exit surveys from a global FMCG organisation over one year, 85% of people leaving the business cited the relationship with their manager as being the main, or a major contributory factor in their decision. This is a multi-billion organisation rated as a top-20 global employer. Most organisations see leadership as something people 'have' or are born with. Few consider it a skill like any other, to be developed over a career, recognising that leaders can be 'bad' (or 'FALSE'), inept (or PASSIVE), or TRUE as we outlined above. One group that sees leadership as a thread woven through the fabric of the organisation is the UK Defence Forces. Leadership here is seen as a vital component of recruitment, promotion and, most importantly, selection for command and is added to professional competence at an equal level. The equivalent percentage leaving the UK Defence Forces (people leaving as a result of their relationship with their Manager) was 1.8%.

## Knowing Where We Are Going

At any time, a TRUE leader ensures that the organisation has clarity and direction - the strategy to succeed. They recognise, develop and engage their people at all times, fostering a team-working environment where everyone has a unity of purpose. In a crisis, this becomes even more important, because the very nature of a crisis such as the pandemic at the moment is that no one really knows how to solve the problem and there is no 'right answer'. A TRUE leader knows that it will take all the brainpower of everyone involved working collaboratively together if the best solution is to be found.

This approach fosters resilience. Resilience is what is called on in the moment of crisis and you invest in resilience when times are good and 'spend' it in moments of crisis.

## Crisis, What Crisis?

A crisis is rarely unforeseen. Bill Gates foresaw the Coronavirus in a 2015 Ted talk. The question is how prepared the team is to meet the challenge. The best way is to develop a team with resilience. This in turn is best achieved through 'TRUE' principles - with clarity of vision, mission and a clear process to inform decisions (T), individuals who are recognised, developed and empowered (R), a uniform sense of purpose (U) and a leader who engenders respect because of the example they set, not the position they hold (E).

In the 2008 financial crisis, an analysis post the event discovered that companies with disengaged (badly led) employees saw their companies reduce by an average of 32%, whilst those with a strong employee engagement increased by 12%. So, if you have invested in leadership, when *All eyes are on you*, you already have a sense of confidence in the capability of the team to deliver in the moment of crisis, as do they in you.

Beyond developing a resilient culture before the crisis occurs, when the crisis hits there are several critical TRUE imperatives. The first is to breathe – to pause, to collect your thoughts. A crisis is rarely a 'one second decision', and thinking creatively under pressure is almost impossible, so remove yourself from the 'limelight' in order to collect the facts and investigate the situation. Establish the time you have to take a decision and use it wisely. Bring together a team of experts who can analyse and inform, listen to their thoughts and use them to identify your options. Be honest and realistic, not over-optimistic – look at the worst-case scenario. Then start thinking creatively about ways in which the crisis could be overcome.

A factory Director in Cairo, faced with the crisis of a fire which destroyed his packaging and warehousing capability gathered his top team together. Whilst a crack 'crisis team' flew from the

US to develop a recovery plan, he had a 2-day session with his team. The first day he told them to relax and not even talk about the fire. On the second they brainstormed solutions. Their 'fix' enabled them to start production 13 days after the fire, 71 days before the recovery plan developed by the crack team, thus saving $3.5m in imported product.

## Don't Panic, Mr Mainwaring

The first reaction of most people is panic. They will see an unending chain of events leading to the destruction of their world. In these early stages, the leader needs above all to remain calm and to send out a positive message. 'We will come through this together', without trying to minimise the seriousness of the situation. Emphasising the 'together' means that we accept the challenge without needing to apologise for the crisis itself.

All eyes are on the leader at this moment. People will be expecting actions to be taken immediately. We know, however, that crises require creative solutions and creativity is difficult when under pressure. The aim is to 'respond' to the challenge, not to 'react'. The next major action for the leader is to gather together their crisis 'team'. This should comprise experts in the disciplines affected by the crisis as well as creative people.

It is critical to have an open and honest debate here, and to explore the very worst outcomes that could happen and then to look at realistic scenarios. Identifying areas that require investigation and tasking members with providing the data and interpretation to enable a balanced decision is a vital stage at this point.

## That Vision thing...

When President Lyndon Johnson was visiting the NASA's Cape Kennedy Space Center during the run up to the Apollo missions, he was taken on a tour of the astronauts' relaxation spaces and comfort facilities to show him how the astronauts would be looked after before and after each mission. Here he bumped into a janitor, whose job it was to keep the communal spaces clean and conduct minor repairs and, out of courtesy, asked him what he was doing. "Helping put a man on the moon" the janitor famously replied.

Now that is having a shared vision, and of all the attributes a TRUE leader needs during a crisis, sharing a vision of the future is absolutely critical and is what people cling to amidst a sea of uncertainty. Leaders may not have all the answers or even know when the crisis will be over, but a well articulated vision tells everyone that if we all work together we can beat this invisible killer and come out the other side. A vision doesn't cost anything, but it is priceless and is the one thing that will give people a sense of direction and unity of purpose.

## Communication Gets You Down

Communication from the leader is a major component in the success of the organisation to handle the crisis. Open, positive and clear communication is vital. On the one hand this needs to outline the situation dispassionately and realistically. On the other, it needs to be inclusive and positive. 'We will get through this together, we have plans in place……

During the intensity of a crisis, it may be necessary to become more authoritarian than is usual. People will understand this because the situation is urgent. Once the crisis is over, remember to revert to reaching out in a more inclusive way.

Enabling challenge and questions from people affected by the crisis is also a huge credibility bonus for the leadership, however, preparation time to respond (rather than react) to the question is vital. That is not to say to learn ways of hiding the truth, more to think of ways to couch the reality in a balanced way. For example the question 'Why is the trend still growing exponentially?' could be answered with 'The trend is exactly as we had predicted at this stage. The situation will get worse before it gets better, however the plan we have put in place will show results in x days and we would expect the numbers to start improving then….'

Empathising with people is fundamental to this communication. Showing that you are with them in their hour of need makes a huge difference to the 'Unity of purpose'.

The Royal family staying in London during the dark days of WW2 had a massive effect on national morale. 'I cannot begin to understand how this must feel for those affected' is even more powerful than 'I understand how you must feel'.

Finally, in terms of communication, thank people. The people that helped in the crisis, the experts, your team. Recognise their efforts and sacrifice.

## Conclusions

A TRUE leader takes positive steps to ensure that people, teams, organisations, nations have a comprehensible vision of where we are going and a unity of purpose to bind us together and get us working collaboratively. He or she will ensure that diversity (in its widest sense) is understood and embraced, so that no section of that entity feels left out and most importantly leads by example.

This is difficult enough to achieve when everything is going well, but never more important than when it isn't, or during a crisis such as the present pandemic.

Passive and False leaders, by contrast, either allow events to happen without any positive interventions to ensure best outcomes (as in the case of passive leadership) or actively act in self interest or the interests of a selective few (false leadership).

The TRUE leader ensures that there is a clarity of vision and decision-making which is empowered through the organisation. They treat their people with respect and delegate to them as much as they are able. They focus on developing their people and stretching their capability as individuals. They are inclusive in their language and intent – 'We're all in this together'.

They develop and foster a spirit of unison.

They themselves set an example of calmness under pressure and the willingness to 'step up to the plate' in times of crisis.

They have the courage to take tough and necessary decisions and the fortitude to see the crisis through.

The TRUE leader can make the critical difference when 'All eyes are on you…'

## About Nigel Allfrey

Nigel Allfrey spent nine years in the Royal Navy, of which six were in the submarine service in both diesel and nuclear submarines and left as a lieutenant in 1987. Nigel then joined Mars Confectionery as a salesman and worked in trade marketing and key accounts management before becoming country manager for Northern Ireland.

Since then, he has spent 24 years in the field of executive development – in commercial skills, leadership and facilitation skills building for over 30 companies including Cadbury, Pepsico, Unilever, Nuqul, The Civil Aviation Authority, Glaxo Smith Kline, Diageo, Asics, Philips, Coors, Telenor and many others.

He has worked in diverse markets and business cultures (35 countries around the world) and has spent over 23,000 hours in front of groups of future leaders, helping them to fulfil their potential. He has also worked from board level to first line management. Nigel is a Master Facilitator.

Aside from facilitation, Nigel has run the Brighton Marathon, is a Community First Responder and enjoys being a grandfather living at Selsey Bill in Sussex.

*https://www.linkedin.com/in/nigel-allfrey-b93aa66/*

## About Mike Davis-Marks

Mike Davis-Marks has over 40 years experience in providing leadership to small and large teams in challenging circumstances. A social entrepreneur since 2012 and now Managing Director of Building Pathways Ltd, a start up providing pre employment training and mentoring to marginalised groups of people, Mike is also a leadership facilitator and coach with  the True Leader Company and a business mentor working with Portsmouth City Council.

Prior to 2012, Mike enjoyed a 36 year career in the Royal Navy as a submarine commander. Highlights include service in seven submarines including navigating and surfacing a submarine to the North Pole (twice), command of the hunter killer submarine, HMS Turbulent, a posting to the British Embassy in Washington DC before, during and after 9/11 and appointments as Director of Recruiting for the Royal Navy and Royal Marines and Director of Public Relations. Outside of the 'day job', Mike is a qualified NLP practitioner and coach, a Past Master of a London Livery Company, Chairman of Trustees for a charity and the immediate past President of an international maritime fellowship, the Anchorites.

*https://www.linkedin.com/in/mike-davis-marks-081b4212/*

*Twitter: jollijacktar*

# How To Thrive, Not Just Survive In 2020 As A Leader

## Robyn Wilson

### How Has My World Changed?

It has been two years since I wrote an article in the chapter on *Emerging Trends* in *Fit for Purpose Leadership #3*. That article discussed the qualities of a Business Intelligent Leader (BIL) and how to become one. I would recommend to you today, that if you have not yet read my article that you take the opportunity to do so after (or before) reading my current thoughts on business leadership in the current world crisis.

Living and working remotely and globally is familiar to me after making a conscious decision to move from 'bricks and mortar' models of business, education and training into the realm of technologically driven alternatives. On attending a national congress in education technology in 2013 I was fortunate to join other leaders, business entrepreneurs and educational specialists in looking at how the world of 'work' and 'life' was rapidly changing for us. I was fortunate to hear the thoughts of leaders such as Simon Sinek and Sir Ken Robinson whom I suggest you follow if you do not already.

Embracing technology seemed a natural thought progression to me. Although I could understand the post GFC (Global Financial Crisis) investment of our Federal Government in 'bricks and mortar' buildings in educational institutions across Australia, it did not seem to me to be a wise investment.

As I predicted these buildings were to become the 'dinosaurs' of the education and technology transformation age. Today many of these buildings stand empty, underutilised or decaying due to inferior quality of materials or other reasons.

Seven years later all face to face learning environments across the education sectors in Australia, if not the world, are being forced to rapidly change their education delivery models. Universities, private vocational and higher education providers were already offering fully online and/or blended models of learning with secondary and primary school learners now following out of necessity in the current social isolation legislated environment.

During these years, I have pivoted, moved across the silos of learning and teaching, training and education, from face to face to blended and back again. I have worked in my own coaching and training business in each of these modes of operation as well as in national leadership positions with large corporate ventures. My clients and students have come from across the globe and we connect in real time via technology.

Technology allowed me to travel and work, at times living in remote rural locations in New South Wales, Victoria, South Australia and Tasmania. To meet the needs of my clients I would often stop in transit in the middle of a tiny town to connect with a remote business client or run an online coaching session using mobile services and platforms.

Being geographically or socially isolated from friends, family, work colleagues and clients is nothing new to me.

So, what has this taught me?

## 1. Resilience Or Mental Toughness

If I have heard the following statement once, I have heard it many times from friends and colleagues who have followed my journey. "You are very resilient, Robyn". In taking risks in life one must be prepared for both the highs and the lows, the successes and the failures, the good and the bad. This I know well.

The question is "How does this differ to Mental Toughness?" and "If you are Resilient are you also Mentally Tough or vice versa?"

Resilience generally means in this context the mental ability of a person to bounce back, to be successful or happy after setback (illness, depression, adversity etc). Mental Toughness on the other hand is a more recently developed concept in the leadership world that does take into consideration a measure of one's ability to be resilient and cope with confidence in the face of adversity allowing a successful outcome.

I refer you to the concept I developed and discussed in *Fit For Purpose Leadership #3* in the chapter on Emerging Trends (2018, p. 129):

A Business Intelligent Leader or a BIL displays all the qualities of a great Human Leader, think Martin Luther King or Sir Winston Churchill. More specifically a collective of Intelligence (IQ), Emotional Intelligence (EQ), Cultural Intelligence (CQ) and Advanced Linguistics (AL).

Your ability to bounce back after this pandemic crisis and the wake of the financial, socio emotional, cultural and political upheaval it leaves will demonstrate true resilience and mental toughness.

## 2. Pivot Or Perish- 'What Was' To 'What Is' Needed

If they cannot make gin, then let them make hand sanitiser. The manufacturing industry has stepped in to meet the shortfall in supply and demand of medical grade products helping to contain the spread of Coronavirus (COVID-19). This is an example of the way in which a business can pivot rather than perish.

I do not have to tell you as a leader in your own right, business or community how to 'suck eggs' but you may now have to decide whether to 'pivot or perish' in the way you lead or do business currently. It is in times of great adversity through economic and financial hardship (GFC or the Great Depression), political (wars, unrest), natural disasters (massive bush fires, floods, tsunamis, cyclones, pandemics) that creativity must be unleashed to come up with unique solutions to massive urgent problems. The consequence of not doing so can be related to my story earlier in this piece about the bricks and mortar 'dinosaurs'. Think about the lack of pivoting in the history of these companies- Kodak, Nokia and HMV compared to others that have such as Shopify, YouTube and Yelp.

So how will you 'Pivot' at this current time? Ask yourself, "What opportunities are there for me at this time?", "What skills, knowledge and or abilities do I have that gives me the edge over others at this time?", "Where can I show leadership, help others or just contribute in my local, wider or global community at this time?" The answers will show you the way.

### 3. Move The Mountain And Make It A Molehill Or Just Make It Transparent And Walk Right Through It.

Now is the time to think differently, laterally and creatively. Use your active imagination to visualise any of the problems that present to you. These are opportunities to create new business ideas and models. See the mountain as a molehill and step over it. Make the mountain transparent and find the obvious solution or a creative one.

Get a team together and brainstorm, Fish Bone, SWOT or PESTEL analyse or use Triple Bottom Line thinking and if in doubt always use the KISS approach to everything. Apply a process framework and stick to it in any approach to solving a problem. Choose one that is proven in getting results and follow through. Your task here is to carry out an internet search on the analysis methods listed above if you do not already know what they are or how to carry them out as I do not have enough word space to fully explain.

Finally, this is the time to stay focused using a data driven framework creating a feedback loop to assist you to stay on track to achieve desired results.

## 4. Your Best Qualities Are Also Your …. Greatest Strengths

You may have heard the saying "that your greatest strengths are also your greatest weaknesses". Now more than ever it is critical to focus on building and promoting your unique strengths. In this uniqueness you will find as a leader, this is your opportunity to shine, lead others and come to the fore in what only seems natural to you but beyond the scope of others.

Take the time to write these down or ask close friends or trusted colleagues what they believe are your strengths and what they perceive you can do in this current situation to lead? Go back and put these into a problem-solving model mentioned in number 3 above.

## 5. Now Is The Time To…

In a quick internet search on "Present Quotes" I found there were over 1000 that immediately popped up on my screen. I do not have the time NOW to list, discuss or share them all with you so that is a task I will suggest you do if feeling unmotivated, in a state of overwhelm or procrastination.

I will ask that you write down the above statement and fill up your page by writing as many alternatives that come into your consciousness. When you stop or pause ask yourself "what else?" and continue this process until there is nothing but a blank space in your mind.

The next step is to prioritise the first five, ten or twenty in order of importance and place a time of completion against them. Make SMART (Specific, Measurable, Achievable, Realistic, Time Based) goals out of these and act.

I trust that you have found some inspiration and direction from my thoughts on this topic and I know that you have the inherent ability to not only survive this current crisis but thrive leading the way. Go well.

- Wilson, R, 'Business Intelligence Leadership' in A. Priestley (ed.), Fit-For-Purpose Leadership #3, Writing Matters Publishing, U.K., 2018, pp 129-135.

## About Robyn Wilson

Robyn is a leadership trainer and coach whose career in education, business management and leadership has spanned 36 years. Since 2013 she has focused on working with established SMEs to develop what she calls Business Intelligence Leadership (BIL) which she writes about in *Fit-For-Purpose Leadership #3* (2018, pp128-135). Most recently while  continuing her study and work in Business Leadership she trained international post graduate students in leadership, business and management to assist them in assimilating into the business community in Australia.

Through her own business development, Robyn discovered the theory and practice of Neuroleadership. This is based on the brain's ability to unlearn and then relearn new behaviours.

Using these techniques Robyn works in a collaborative approach to assist others to break through their barriers to achieve success and excellence.

Connect with Robyn

*robyn@robynwilson.com.au*

# What Leadership Looks Like In A Pandemic

## Baiju Solanki

These are unprecedented times, but we as a society are not strangers to unprecedented situations.

Individually, more than likely, we have all encountered change or disruption in our lives. That could be at work, in your personal life or a social situation.

The difference now is that WE ALL are in the SAME situation. Meaning that all of us have to adapt to new times and a new way of being.

Being in lockdown means we spend more time in our heads. Spending all that time within ourselves requires us to be disciplined, focused and believe in ourselves.

This is where I think true leadership is shown.

There are three parts to Leadership:-

1.  **Self- Leadership** - Train your thoughts, Detach from outcome, Own your space

2.  **Leadership to Serve** - Understand your audience, Create something bigger than you, solve a problem

3.  **Leadership to Create a New Way Of Life** - Learn how to adapt, Take that risk now, Take massive action

## Characteristics of Self-Leadership

In these acute times, there is a lot of self-reflection and inner work. All the so-called normal 'outs' that we would normally use as excuses not to work on our inner leadership are no longer available.

What are the excuses we used before?

- Not enough time?
- Will it make a difference?
- Don't know how to start?

Now we have the time, if we use it properly. You will only know IF it makes a difference if you do it and the best thing to do is just start, that is what leadership is about.

Three ways that you can start to develop your Self-Leadership:

**1. Learn How to Train Your Thoughts** - You are what you think, you are also what you feel. Self-leadership always starts with your mindset. Your mindset is determined by your thoughts and feelings. The situation out there that you cannot directly control Is either happening to you or for you. When you shift your thoughts to it happening for you, you take control. Your perspective changes when you change your thoughts. You see things differently. What can you choose to see in a lockdown, actually in any challenging situation? When you see things differently IT CHANGES EVERYTHING. You have to control your mind, that is self-leadership…what does that look like?

- You don't give in to temptation
- You don't procrastinate
- You respond and not react
- You don't attach yourself to outcomes
- You take TOTAL responsibility

Now is the time to take a stand, whatever is happening around you. Now is the time to focus on who you want to BE in this situation. Because this will decide who you to want be, and when you decide what you want, you can get clarity on what you need to do. If you do this for yourself, you can then start to do this for others.

**2. Detach From the Outcome** - I use this acronym with my clients NATO. What this means is Not Attached To Outcome.

Before this situation occurred we had many expectations, now we may still have expectations, but the rules of engagement have changed. If you are reading this AFTER the lockdown has been lifted and we are out at the other end ... these principles still apply. When we are attached to an outcome, we are not present to the task at hand. If you are not present to the task at hand, then we are not giving ourselves our best chance to achieve the best outcome. When you develop this muscle of detaching yourself from the outcome your leadership is free to grow and you can serve others better, we talk more about this in the next part. When the outcome doesn't matter, the pressure is off. You have no expectations and aren't scared to make a mistake. Self-leadership is about context, which takes us back to the previous point about training your thoughts. When you train your thoughts your context of leadership changes.

You start from who you are and focus on the process and detach yourself from the outcome.

**3. Own Your Space** – Self-leadership is about *certainty*. When you own your own space you project certainty. What you are saying to the world is these are my values and I am comfortable with that. People want to know from you that you can hold the space and working on your inner game gives you that. Owning your space is about authenticity where there is no ego involved, you believe in yourself and in times of uncertainty you are giving the world some certainty. Your focus, when you own your space will be 100% on serving others and not worrying about looking good and scared of failure.

## Leadership To Serve

The second part of leadership, however probably the most impactful in these times is serving others. Leadership to serve means IT'S ALL ABOUT THEM. This is how you create other leaders.

When you show up for others, two things occur...

1. You take the pressure off yourself

2. You show others how to lead purely from your actions

So how can you start to lead and to serve where it doesn't look inauthentic and is genuine.

Here are three ways:

**1. Understand Your Audience** - Whoever you are leading, make sure you understand what they are dealing with. How can you do this? Ask them. We are blessed with technology at our fingertips. We can ask either directly by phoning them, sending out surveys, conducting polls and using social media posts and stories. One big failure of leadership to serve is assumptions about who you are serving. When you make assumptions about your market place and how they want to serve, you are coming from your ego and not from a place of complete service. Doing the inner work around self-leadership naturally changes your focus to serve others, because you are taking care of yourself and you don't serve from a self-serving position.

**2. Make It Bigger Than You** - In times when we are all uncertain about the future, the immediate behaviour is self-preservation and survival. Now the way to lead is to make it not about you and make it bigger than you. It could be an inspiration, solving a problem, serving your community or being there for your clients. The world needs leaders who look at the problems that exist in the world and come up with solutions. When you lead to serve, your lead without ego. When you lead to make an impact, you lead to make a difference.

**3. Solve a Real Problem** - There is a problem in the world now that didn't exist years ago, months ago, weeks ago, even days ago. If you are reading this during the pandemic, we are confronted every day with new problems. You now have to be the leaders who are offering and leading on solutions to these problems. One of the best ways to do this is through collaboration. You are reading this chapter as part of a book that was created through collaboration. This book was conceived to serve you, the reader, to be a more effective leader. This book was not 'needed' a few weeks ago. Now a new problem exists and so new solutions are needed. Again if you are reading this after the virus has been dealt with, these principles still apply. Now go a seek what real problems exist now that you are the leader we are all looking for.

## Leadership To Create A New Way Of Life

Whatever your opinion, the world will be very different post-pandemic. We have never experienced anything like this, it has affected the entire world. This will not only have an impact on well-being but mental health and the economy. There will be casualties, sadly people have lost their lives and businesses will close. So whatever type of leader you are or were before, now is your opportunity to be a leader to create a new way of life.

Here are three ways to be that leader:-

**1. Learn How to Adapt** - Now more than ever your leadership is about adapting to the new way of working. This is the time you have to re-evaluate where you are, what you do and what you want to achieve. When you adapt effectively you look at the world differently, you assess your skill set and talent and you allow your thinking to see new possibilities and opportunities. Whatever your industry the rules of engagement have changed. For some of you when this time passes, we just go again. However, for a lot of people, you will have to do things differently. The time to adapt is now. How can you do this effectively?

- Know your vision, your vision before COVID-19 can be the same now, the execution is now different, go back to your vision and values and start from there

- Take a step back - take your time and don't rush. Time is the one commodity that we have now and so use it effectively

- Plan and Strategise - map out your solutions to the new problem that is occurring. Solve a real problem that exists now, not the ones six months ago.

**2. Take That Risk Now** - Now more than ever is a good time to take calculated risks. This is not a time to play safe, but it is also not a time to be restless in your actions. In 2007 I took the biggest calculated risk of my life and left my well paid, established corporate job. I didn't know it at that time but I left three months before the 2008 economic crash. But it didn't affect me as much as it should have. Why you may ask?

There were three main reasons…

- My naivety, I didn't know any different
- When I left my job I knew who and what I wanted to do
- I trusted myself to deal with any challenges that came to me

Thankfully, although I have had some trying times, near on 13 years, notwithstanding a pandemic, I am still here and serving.

**3. Take Massive Action** - This is not a time for timid slow actions. Yes-you need to prepare. Yes-you need to take your time. Yes-you need to adapt to the new world, but do not stop in taking massive action every day. The book you are reading now is a result of adapting to these times, looking at what the market needs and how as leaders we can serve that market. Within a few weeks getting these articles written, formatted and published so you can be the leader you need to be in these challenging times.

## About Baiju Solanki

## CEO & Founder of EnSpirit Global

Baiju is the CEO and founder of EnSpirit Global: a platform that serves to inspire, educate and connect the entrepreneurial spirit in all of those who wish to live their best life. In addition an award-winning businessman and TEDx speaker.

A trained psychologist, lecturer, speaker and author, he empowers people to achieve their power. Using his skills as a trainer, teacher and coach he aims to transform the world through teaching entrepreneurial skills to business people, students and employees through the EnSpirit platform.

As a former Businessman of The Year, and property investor, his experience extends beyond the realm of enterprise.

Baiju is also an author of #1 Amazon Best Seller *Change Your Game: How to To Achieve Your Potential as an Entrepreneur* and *Create the Life You Desire* and *I'm An Entrepreneur - Get Me Out of Here',* a selection of interviews with entrepreneurs who talk about the keys to success.

*www.EnSpirit.Global*

*www.ChangeYourGameBook.com*

*www.ChangeYourGameAccelerator.com*

## Baiju Solanki's Social Media Links

*https://twitter.com/BaijuSolanki*

*https://www.facebook.com/baiju.solanki*

*https://www.linkedin.com/in/baijusolanki/*

*https://www.instagram.com/baijusolanki/*

*https://www.youtube.com/user/baijusolanki/videos*

*TEDx Talk*

*https://www.youtube.com/watch?v=HA-TFRXRWPY&t=48s*

# Good Day, This Is Your Captain Speaking ...

## Louise Jupp

### Introduction

[Bear with me, I acknowledge this is perhaps a hackneyed phrase, but it captures the essence of leadership and, arguably, is what we need now and especially for the future, as I shall describe below.]

I have huge respect for pilots, military or civilian.

I count myself very fortunate in that much of my ground school instruction for my drone licensing training was with the Chief Instructor at a local, highly respected flying school. I was essentially given a level of instruction equivalent to the Private Pilot's License course. I was also able to complete my radio telephony practical exam in the air at the controls of a Savannah.

This was a thrilling way for me to complete my training for the approved Remote Pilot's (Drone) License that I obtained shortly after. Importantly, it brought home to me several key features about aviation that have considerable relevance about the leadership qualities that 'we' need to see us through these globally challenging times and into the future.

### Our Trust of the Pilot

At the start of your flight, the words 'Good day, this is your Captain speaking' typically invoke a sense of comfort.

Of course. Why not? It's the Captain. By the very title, you believe that someone qualified and experienced is at the controls. You also believe that they know what they are doing, where they are going and they will get you there safely (and, hopefully, on time).

Or more succinctly, you trust the pilot. Implicitly!

This is interesting given that you are unlikely to know the pilot personally or had a chance to study their flying history before boarding the aircraft! You may argue that you have no choice but to trust the pilot once you are buckled in and heading down the runway. Still, you want to trust them because it helps you feel better in your relatively vulnerable state as a passenger.

Come what may, you inherently trust that the pilot has had extensive training, accrued long hours of experience and is fit to fly. You trust that they are well prepared for the trip, have the right equipment and, importantly, they are prepared for any emergency situations that may arise.

Leadership is wholly centered on *trust*.

As a pilot, this demands an acceptance of responsibility to those putting their trust in you. It is reflected in the extensive training undertaken and in the rules of the air. In becoming a pilot, you are accepting full responsibility for your actions on the ground and in the air.

We look to leaders we can trust. We want to trust that they are prepared, know what to do, care about us and are doing what's best for us all. This is never more so important than during an emergency situation such as a pandemic.

We need our leaders to accept responsibility in the same way.


## Cool. Calm. Collected

'Cool, calm, collected' is another hackneyed phrase, but again there is an element of truth in it from a leadership perspective and especially for pilots where situations are far from normal.

Trust, as we all know, is earned through actions. The actions of pilots in an emergency tend to stand out as an example of the leadership qualities we need to see in the pandemic and in any future crisis.

Pilots operate in a harsh environment where time is short and gravity invariably has the last word. The ability to be cool, calm and collected in an emergency is, in its own right, essential to survival. It gives the pilot more time to react and prompts others to keep their composure so that everyone can work towards the preferred common goal of having an equal number of takeoffs and landings!

So often, where the pilot seems to have performed a miraculous feat to avoid total disaster, their persona during the crisis has been described as being:

- Stolid
- Stoic
- Confident
- Focused
- Well-trained
- Concerned for crew and passengers

However, the performance is not just a product of character and temperament. It is also a product of rigorous training. Pilots are constantly preparing for the emergency situations that could happen, practicing the procedures and manoeuvres for scenarios they hope not to face. But they practice them repeatedly nonetheless so that their responses become second nature and can be delivered skillfully, with confidence and stoicism when required.

In most cases, the pilots who have prevented major loss of life and been labeled heroes or heroines by the media, do not accept this label. They were doing their job. It was their responsibility as the 'Pilot in Command' to use their 'knowledge, experience and skill to avoid dangerous situations' and look after their crew and passengers.[1]

The apparent absence of outward fear from the pilot is a consequence of knowing what can go wrong, what can be done and acting accordingly when the time comes. This in turn engenders confidence and calm in those on board and on the ground.

The memorable calm announcement, 'Houston we've had a problem' by Jack Swigert and Jim Lovell from the gravely stricken Apollo 13 is the epitome of years of training, as was the measured response of NASA's Mission Control.

In times of crisis we want our leaders to exhibit these traits. As in an aircraft in distress, bravado at the podium has no value in resolving problems. Statements that calm either individual or collective fears; prevent confusion; or invoke collective support for actions are required.

Generally, many leaders have the right character and temperament to pilot their nations through difficult times. However, they do not have the training or experience to respond to this type of emergency situation. Significantly, they do not appear to have a manual of standard, well-informed procedures to reach for or the equivalent of a reliable Mission Control to consult.

This is evident in the different ways countries have been prepared for or subsequently reacted to the crisis. It is also evident in the mixed advice being currently issued, such as whether face masks should be worn by the public or not. This inconsistency is undermining our leaders' ability to offer comfort and confidence by their proposed actions and, in some cases, garner public support for the actions needed.

As in aviation, leaders need to be ready to take the right steps in an emergency. Allowing for the transient nature of politicians' tenure at the top negating the value of extensive training, it is important that leaders have a clear strategy or manual of procedures, at the very least. I will return to this point under 'Post Accident Investigations'.

## Aviate. Navigate. Communicate.

The three-word axiom for guiding a pilot's priorities should an emergency situation develop in the air, is 'Aviate, Navigate, Communicate.'

The primary goal above all else is for the pilot to gain control of the aircraft. The next step is for the pilot to identify where they are and where they can land safely. The final step is to communicate with air traffic control, to let them know their problem, position, plans and needs, and then with the crew and passengers.

This can all happen very quickly, but the order is critical. At first this may seem back-to-front, but it is common sense: get control, know your next steps and let others know.

Similarly, it may be necessary to go through several iterations of this approach if conditions change on board. Nonetheless, controlling the aircraft is paramount.

This axiom has often been suggested as a useful model for general application in stressful situations in business for corporate leaders and managers. I think it has merit for this pandemic and for future pandemics.

The primary focus of the response to the pandemic has been to 'flatten the curve' or slow the rate of infection, the equivalent of 'aviate'. The purpose being to reduce the strain on medical services, gather resources and create time for research to identify a vaccine or cure. All of which are geared towards reducing the loss of life.

The three-step approach has, to a certain degree, been applied by a number of leaders, but not necessarily in the right order! Or with the quality of information on where we are, where we are going, how we are going to get there or with the level of clear communication we would expect in the air.

We need leaders to grasp the essence of the emergency and gain control as soon as the warning lights flash and alarms sound. We need leaders to make informed decisions and apply prepared strategies to steer us to safety.

It is noteworthy that when an engine failure occurs on take-off, you are taught to 'crash straight ahead'. To turn, will cause a loss of lift with, probably, drastic consequences. Your chances of survival are greatly improved by aiming to land straight ahead and using what lift you have to land with more control.

We need leaders to set and keep to a clear course. We need leaders to communicate with and be guided by a team of experts, the equivalent of air traffic control or Mission Control. Finally, we need leaders to communicate with their 'crew and passengers' through dedicated channels with clear messages on what is happening, what is being done, where we are going and how we will get there.

## Post Accident Investigations

An investigation always follows an aviation accident or incident. Conducted by experts, the investigation aims to learn from the accident, identify measures to reduce the risk of repetition and ultimately improve air safety.

The causes of the accident and sequence of events are identified. The final report typically recommends improvements to training, cockpit procedures and maintenance procedures. The investigations are not just to 'blame' the aircrew or ground crew, but to learn and improve.

Hard lessons have been learned over the decades of civilian and military flight but these have been converted into improved regulations, equipment design, procedures and training. Today's highly regulated aviation industry has a solid safety record, which demonstrates the effectiveness of a strategy of continuous review and improvement.

This pandemic demanded a global response. However, the response has not been globally consistent or coordinated. This, in turn, has caused different national outcomes, confusion, panic buying, blatant disregard of the risks,economic hardship and social unrest.

Thus, the response to the next pandemic must be based on a coherent strategy and action plan for a coordinated response by all stakeholders. This strategy and action plan must, in turn, be developed by experts from a comprehensive review of how this pandemic was (mis)managed.

We need to learn from this pandemic so that leaders and communities can benefit from the implementation of effective procedures and coordinated responses to future similar global scenarios.

It is imperative that our leaders have a single path to follow, trained staff to implement their instructions and the appropriate resources, if we are to react as a global community to effectively manage global threats. This will undoubtedly call for unprecedented levels of leadership, cooperation and non-partisan engagement and support, as well as public commitment.

## Conclusions

So far, we have seen leadership of mixed quality.

In aviation, pilots are largely defined by their actions. Good pilots, are highly trained, follow the routine, know their craft, follow the rules, and prepare for the worst. When the worst does occur, they typically react instinctively. In addition, they have resources to hand as back up in the form of manuals, procedures, checklists and ultimately guidance from air traffic control. These actions maximise the safety of crew, passengers and others in the air and on the ground.

Aviation is about safety. Leaders would do well to emulate the aviation industry's approach to emergency situations for developing a coherent, coordinated and effective response to future pandemics.

- Pratt JM (2012). Private Pilot's License Course PPL5 Human Factors Flight Safety (AFE).

## About Louise Jupp

Louise Jupp is the best-selling author of *Precision Farming from Above* and editor of the best-selling *Drone Professional* series. She is a licensed drone pilot with over 370 flying hours and drone instructor. She has a Master's Degree in Environmental Science and has over 28 years experience in environmental impact assessment and management in the UK, Europe and across Africa.

She is the owner of Terreco Aviation, a consultancy for the professional use of drones in agriculture and sustainable land management community, based in South Africa. Louise recognises the powerful data-gathering and management tool commercial drone systems provide across many sectors. The power of commercial drone system lies in the ability to rapidly provide a broad range of high-quality actionable data at the right time, enabling managers to make the right decisions with the right resources at the right locations at the right time.

With a passion for the professional use of drones in land management and agriculture in particular, Louise believes commercial drone systems are fundamental to all farmers increasing their productivity and to helping nations meet rising global demand for food production in more sustainable ways.

*Http://linkedin.com/in/louise-jupp*

*Louise@terrecoaviation.com*

*Www.terrecoaviation.com*

# High-Value Connections For Business Health In Turbulent Times

## Matthew Newnham

Suffice it to say, our current environment is turbulent, deeply worrying and set to be with us for months. And yet, as a respected leader recently said, "We don't agonise, we organise."

So what specifically can we business owners do to keep attracting and retaining clients effectively in the current environment and beyond, even remotely?

The simplest and most powerful way I know is to increase the value of your relationships with your prospects and clients. You have two options.

Firstly, you may need to adapt your service to meet the current market conditions. However, the odds are also pretty high that communicating (online) with more value to your prospects and clients will not only be required, but get you a higher ROI. So, how do you do that?

## Where Do Most Online Communications Typically Fail?

When you're looking online for timely help, what are you finding? How often do you encounter content and messages that deliver high value, add trust and relate specifically to you and your current situation?

Most business owners I talk with find far too much of this instead:

- "Fluffy", generic or "boilerplate", with little or no value
- "Look at me" - focused on the author and their business
- Worthy but dull information that misses the mark
- "TL;DR" (too long; didn't read) content (and messages)
- Unsolicited or inappropriate pitches (blatant or subtle, polite or not)

In 'normal' times, these judgements are made in the blink of an eye. But now, this happens far faster, like a razor-sharp scythe slicing through dry wheat, discarding it just as quickly.

## What High-Value Relationships Really Demand

Suppose you have a problem that you really want to fix. What if you go online and find someone providing credible information that actually helps you make immediate progress towards solving your problem?

And what if that content is offered freely, without hiding it behind a demand for your email or wrapped around an immediate sales pitch?

You'll be far more likely to trust that person and consider them as a valuable resource, right? And you'll be far more likely to buy from them. As marketing guru Seth Godin says:

"The purpose of being creative, the purpose of solving problems, is so that you can generously give those insights away. Because people like it when you do that, and they'll become more connected with you. And if your work meets the promises you make for it, they will trust you more."

## Gaps And Opportunities

You'd think useful content like this would be the norm, but that's not what we find. In fact, "88 percent of 400 business buyers believe online content plays a major to moderate role in vendor selection, yet just nine percent of respondents think of vendors as trusted sources of content." - CMO Council report: Making Content Marketing Convert (2020).

So what can we do to ensure that our content creates high-value relationships that attract and retain more clients and revenue? The advice that follows is based on what works for our clients globally and other thought leaders who focus on delivering high-value content.

## Two Vital Fundamentals Before We Start Writing

First and foremost, clear positioning is absolutely vital if you want to create higher-value business relationships via online content and messaging. Clear, high-value positioning is enhanced by content. But even great content is compromised if the business creating it is positioned vaguely or isn't focused on that business's highest value in the marketplace.

Note: The vast majority of us should be positioned around just one strong area of value.

Next, you need to know which content strategy you're following. Most online content and messaging is focused on generating demand rather than creating and nurturing relationships. The former is a short-term tactic to get the phones to ring. The latter is a longer-term strategy aimed at building a continual flow of prospects and customers.

Demand gen marketing can work, but it's harder to generate a quick flow of leads (and sales) without pre-existing trusted relationships. Plus, the success rate can be very hit and miss, requiring you to hold your nerve under time and cost pressures. In my experience, most of us do not have the skills, resources and temperament to succeed with this strategy.

Happily, any business can learn to create and maintain valued conversations with their audience, based on high-value content. With the heightened focus on value and urgency across the business landscape, choosing wisely carries a lot more weight for your business.

## What Do I Write?

This is what stops so many from creating content (or writing their book etc). In our case, however, the answer is simple - answer these questions:

- What are the most pressing problems that my ideal prospects and clients want help with right now?
- What barriers are they encountering in trying to solve those problems?

Provide clear, simple answers to these questions, tackling one central idea for each piece of content (or message). You're aiming for maximum practical value, ease of consumption (keep it short) and simplicity of use for busy people under pressure. If you need to create a short series of connected pieces, do that if it's engaging and value-add.

You may also be wondering about writing content on mindset, especially since there's so much of it out there. But be careful: much of it conveys a warm, fuzzy feeling at best, and fails to pass the "So what?" test. Your best bet is to focus on solving specific problems.

Note: Most people get hung up on the words to use. But in any writing, you want to put most of your thinking into figuring out the main idea and the hook for your story. Once you have those, it's far easier to craft the specific words (for which you can always seek help).

However, when it comes to your words, it pays to work hard on what I call The Three R's:

1. **Relevance** - Is this really what my audience cares about and will find of value now?

2. **Relatability** - Am I using clear language that they feel genuinely speaks to them? (As a rule, I find it best to remember how you would speak to a valued friend.)

3. **Recurrence** - To really build trust and grow your value, you need to be consistently seen to be adding value. Your content is like a garden: tend it and it will feed you.

## Further Essential Tips For High-Value Online Content And Messaging

### Become a genuine trusted advisor

One of the biggest problems people face online is not knowing who to trust. Your content and messaging can help them to solve their problems. But they will spot your intentions very quickly if you're more focused on selling than providing genuine help.

### Don't worry that providing valued content means you'll end up working for free

On the contrary, this approach actually positions you with more value, because you provide clarity (assuming it's based on true expertise and authority in your field). Plus, when you show someone what they can do to solve their problem, they very often will ask for your paid help to show them how to do it, or to do it for them.

### Keep it bite-sized wherever possible

As brand strategist Donald Miller teaches, most marketing takes far too much time and effort to consume. In other words, it contains far too many calories. Your content and messages need to be nutritious, but quick to consume and put into action.

## You do not have to be everywhere

We've all seen social media personalities who manage to have tons of content on multiple platforms. But let's get real: those people expend a ton of time, effort and money to do that. The good news, a focused and effective strategy, consistently well executed on one powerful platform can work wonders. (LinkedIn is by far my preferred recommendation - you can be viewed as "being everywhere" just there.)

## Personality counts - but mostly theirs, not ours

I highly advise thinking beyond marketing metrics to consider the personality types of your prospects and clients. Find a framework that you trust and test it out. (I've specialised in this approach in branding and content for the past decade and clients really value the insights they get from this. See the links below for more information.)

## Your Natural Route to Thriving in Any Environment

The concepts I've shared here have been proven to work for business owners around the world, in a variety of markets. (And they'll work just as well in your live conversations as they will in your online content and messaging.)

Your expertise and your ability to share it via high-value online content and messaging presents a golden opportunity to do well by doing good.

Thanks very much for reading, and very best wishes for a successful and thriving business that meets your needs, fulfils your dreams and helps make the world a better place.

## About Matthew Newnham

Matthew Newnham is a brand positioning and online content specialist who helps business owners clarify their value and become respected thought leaders. This enables them to grow their business credibly and naturally, with far less risk.

He has been a lifelong student of how we communicate with each other, starting with his days as an air cadet and officer, then as a corporate change management consultant and since 2011, as a brand positioning and communications specialist.

Along with his great friend Nicholas Haines, he is co-founder at *Five Institute*, home of *The Vitality Test*. Along with Nick's 50,000 one-on-one consultations over 38 years and Matthew's branding consultations with business owners around the world, *The Vitality Test* (created by Nick) has been completed by over 20,000 people around the world and they tell us it's the most insightful and valuable personality test they've ever experienced.

In his leisure time, Matthew is a keen club-level runner and Scottish Masters medallist, competing in the 800m, 1500m and mile (and for his sins, cross country!).

Learn more about his brand positioning and communications that connect at https://repositionme.com/

Connect with him on LinkedIn at:

*https://www.linkedin.com/in/matthewnewnham/*

Learn about your personality type and how it can transform your business (take the free online Vitality Test, then contact Matthew via LinkedIn for a personalised walkthrough):

*https://www.fiveinstitute.com/*

# Leadership In The Time Of Crisis

## Suparna Malhotra

It's the spring of 2020 and we are facing a global pandemic and crisis the like of which people of our generation have never experienced. It has caused us to question everything, from the way we live to the way we lead and manage.

Thge pandemic is a global tragedy. However, one impact of the devastation it will leave in its wake, is the opportunity it will provide not only for leaders, but for us all to evolve. A chance to rise to the challenge of leading through a crisis and shape the future. How you respond now will determine your legacy.

The need for appropriate leadership is immense right now. People are questioning how authoritative a stance a government can take in a modern, democratic society like the UK. They can follow a leader by choice, or alternatively adapt a parent-like approach and enforce a following. Early attempts at leaving us a choice included vague messaging from the government, which failed to galvanise the British public to make the right choices and self-isolate, so a more authoritative tone needed to be taken.

This raises the question regarding what is appropriate leadership at a time of crisis. The very fabric of modern leadership is transforming. Does this mean independent think-ing with personal responsibility is rendering 'taking orders' a thing of the past?

The answer is not cut and dry. Leaders need to be agile and

adaptable to situations and context. Authority is no longer bestowed upon us, it is earned through trust, integrity and credibility. People may be willing to follow authority that they deem to be rooted in a shared mission and vision. with added compassion. Angela Merkel, the German chancellor issued a clear and concise message to the nation, and acted decisively in shutting businesses and public spaces down early, thereby treating the population as capable of responsibility, and showing she was in this with them.

Credibility is cultivated through trusted relationships, which in turn create safety. Creating the right environment prior to a crisis will permit others to comply, without rebellious resistance. In his book, How to Win, former England rugby coach Sir Clive Woodward (or just Clive, as he prefers to be addressed), described formulating ground rules from the start with his team. These rules included respect for one another and a commitment to being number 1. The proof is clearly in the pudding as the team went on to win the 2003 Rugby World Cup.

## Lead With Care

Achievements of that calibre are built on relationships. Crucially this means relationships with self as well as with others. Warren Duffet was not wrong when he said, 'the most important investment you can make is in yourself'. Generally, the most under accomplished task in one's to-do list is genuine self-care that empowers you to place your well-being as a top priority. What if compassion for self were the bottom line? It reminds me of the old adage of when you are asked to place your own oxygen mask on first before helping another in an emergency onboard a flight. As counterintuitive as that may seem, you are of no use to anyone if you are unconscious.

With much of the world's population in lockdown, self-care is now a significant priority. Those who exercise regularly are amping it up, increasing the frequency. Indeed, in many cases, physical fitness has become an important part of even a novice's day. By being unable to go out, we are invited to go in. Busy schedules and the need to rush meant there was no time for this. Energy was always put towards achieving the hard bottom line of profit.

Gordon Ramsay was not the only business owner to dismiss hundreds of staff members due to a knee-jerk reaction from a place of panic. Until you find a way through the fear, it is not possible to find compassion even for yourself. Without reserves of inner resources there is a vulnerability to making mistakes or burning out.

When fear and anxiety take over we are thrust into our primitive fight or flight response. The pre-frontal cortex, necessary for rational thought, goes 'offline' leaving a great deal of room for error. The panic buying and empty shelves recently seen in supermarkets across the world are a clear ex-ample of that in action.

Fortunately, our culture is now beginning to grasp that physical, as well as mental fitness is the recipe for resilience. Organisations such as the American car manufacturer, Chevron and Google offer gyms to help their employees care for their physical health, as well as a variety of facilities that look after mental health and well-being. The success of an organisation stems from its people, as my father who is now a retired business owner always said to me. One of a leader's top concerns needs to be the growth, development and welfare of their staff.

This is evident in how Management style has evolved in sport. Gone are the days when boots were flung across the changing rooms by managers after a loss. Care, respect and trust in the individual is met with loyalty, dedication and the desire to win shiny trophies, as is evident in the ethos of Liverpool FC team manager, Jurgen Klopp.

### Let Go Of Sh*T

In March 2018 I held a workshop on dealing with imposter syndrome at the Google offices in London. However, despite the event's success, rather than benefit from it I was engulfed in my own version of the imposter syndrome. The existence of a real threat has opened up the opportunity for us all to discard those irrational and untrue and self-made ones.

It's time to shake off perfectionism's relentless grip, the imposter's cruel voice and learn that our true value is not in what we do, but in who and how we are. Self-isolation, social-distancing and a countrywide lockdown is teaching us the value and the skill to just 'be'. We have been forced to slow down seeing that there is nowhere to rush to. We are invited to face ourselves, for where else can we hide? Through the fear, anxiety and uncertainty, we have been stripped bare to our core. The very mettle the leaders of our countries and organisa-tions, and indeed us all are made of is ex-posed, illuminating the importance of caring for ourselves.

This was still apparent two years later, as the coronavirus crisis hit home in Europe and I was on holiday in Tulum, Mexico. What was intended to be a week of deep relaxation soon became stressful. The fear and anxiety I felt left me incapable of deciding the right course of action for getting home. Incapa-ble of finding a rational way of dealing with the fact that there was imminent danger that could strike me or my family, all in different countries, at any time, it took a few days to shake myself out of panic mode and into a state of calm. It was only when I reached this point that I could make a rational decision.

When fear and anxiety take over we are thrust into our primitive fight or flight response. The pre-frontal cortex, necessary for rational thought, goes 'offline' leaving a great deal of room for error. The panic buying and empty shelves recently seen in supermarkets across the world are a clear ex-ample of that in action.

Gordon Ramsay was not the only business owner to dismiss hundreds of staff members due to a knee-jerk reaction from a place of panic. Until you find a way through the fear, it is not possible to find compassion even for yourself. Without reserves of inner resources there is a vulnerability to making mistakes or burning out.

## Lead with connection

When have we seen scientists across the globe collaborating as they have in the race to find a vaccine that puts an end to this pandemic? Never has there been a time where competition rules were relaxed to allow essential businesses to work relentlessly to allow us access to food and basics.

Children are enjoying having parents at home and online access is rekindling friendships the world over. Life's pace is slowing down. This is an opportunity to cultivate and nurture the teams we already have from a place of compassion. We are seeing that the world is more connected than ever.

The shifting business landscape shows a trend towards a decentralised management system. The traditional, hierarchical, top-down management style is falling off the shelf, making room for the latest version, that requires trust, influence and collaboration.

Some are using this crisis to strengthen their grasp on power. Many are stepping in to provide the kind of care and reassurance so many of us have needed to get through this. I always ask my clients, what kind of legacy they want to leave as a leader. Will it be, leading with a stick? Or a carrot, in the form of empowerment and trust? Which, will you choose?

## References

- Woodward, C. (2019). How to Win. Hodder & Stoughton Ltd

## About Suparna Malhotra

Suparna is an executive leadership coach who enables her clients to achieve greater self-awareness and lasting results. Clients walk away with a clear vision and ability to develop sustain high performing and resilient teams.

Suparna is also an ardent, long standing Liverpool FC supporter.

*www.suparnaway.com*

*www.linkedin.com/in/suparnamalhotra*

*@thesuparnaway*

# Strategic Leadership

## Jim McLaughlin

What do Thomas Edison, Walt Disney and Bill Gates have in common? They all started their businesses during a recession/depression. As did the founders of Dropbox, Slack, Pinterest, Uber and Groupon. The Rich Lists are populated with stories of people who survived extreme business shocks and went on to thrive. Insurer Hiscox[1] discovered that businesses founded in the financial recession in Europe had higher growth rates, higher profitability and more ambitious strategies just a few years later.

Now that might be comforting for pre-starts but less so for established businesses who have been affected with customers, employees, landlords, suppliers and investors to satisfy. As well as attending to the emotional needs of their people, leaders must also help to navigate the ship through the storm by facilitating, communicating and executing the strategy calmly and decisively. No matter how good you are at the pastoral side of leadership, your people want direction and clarity, security and hope.

Many heads are better than yours alone. Assemble multiple brains; gather your best strategic thinkers into a group that is not too big and unwieldy. Supplement it with external people (e.g. your accountant, advisers) if helpful. If your business is very small and there are no natural fellow strategists, perhaps join forces with others in a similar situation. Your job as a leader is to structure the strategic thinking and co-ordinate actions.

If you are running a big business, you will certainly benefit from creating a timetable of activities and from creating a running action plan using project and tasks management tools such as Monday, Trello or Asana.

The first objective of any business negatively impacted by a shock like a pandemic is survival. Nobody knows precisely what is going to happen next so you need to prepare by thinking of this situation as evolving across three timeframes, each of which has its own objectives and points of focus:

| Phase | Objectives |
| --- | --- |
| Emergency phase | Survival and operational resilience: employee wellbeing, cash (income), cash (expenditure), cash (funding) |
| Restart phase | Recovery: proposition, operations, pricing, opportunities |
| Long term phase | Refocus: new needs, products and services, channels to market, innovation opportunities |

Getting ahead of the changes in your external environment will give you maximum time to adapt, develop and innovate.

The emergency phase can be planned for using the following key questions:

1. What do we need to do to ensure the wellbeing of our people?

2. What is our actual financial position right now and forecast over the next 13 weeks/a quarter ahead?

3. What should we do to maximise cash into the business (invoicing, cash chasing, grants and temporary payment holidays)?

4. What should we do to secure financing to meet our needs?

5. What should we do to bring forward and otherwise secure sales?

6. What should we do to reduce costs without damaging our business?

7. What should we do to refocus the business on delivering value profitably?

8. What should we stop doing because it creates insufficient value or consumes cost?

9. What should we start doing to optimise our financial position and set us up for the recovery?

You also need to be thinking strategically about the recovery period and beyond. Here are three suggested recovery scenarios against which to generate insights and ideas:

## 1. The V Shaped Bounce

Some commentators are suggesting that because other fundamentals (GDP growth, industrial activity, corporate profitability, bank liquidity) were in reasonable shape prior to the lockdown that the economy and consumers could quickly recover confidence in an exuberant expression of freedom to shop, dine and travel. This could see a relatively short-lived recession where furloughed workers are re-hired and everything starts up again as it was before.

## 2. The Hockey Stick

Having looked at the aftermath of 16 sharp and sudden economic shocks such as war, earthquake, tsunami and other natural disasters, the recovery pattern looks remarkably similar. The sharp drop is followed by a curve of varying radiuses and a climb out of the shock. The recovery may be measured in years.

## 3.The Victorian Bath

The third scenario is a deep and prolonged recession leading to high unemployment, falling demand, a sharp rise in insolvencies, tightening of credit, rises in sovereign debt, bank crises and collapse in the value of multiple asset classes such as equities, property and bonds. Some are saying that the unprecedented suddenness and totality of the economic shutdown will trigger systemic effects that could lead to a depression.

You don't need to buy into the most gloomy scenario in order to perform thought experiments with it. Airplane passengers who watch the safety announcements and plan their route out are more likely to survive. Scenario thinking encourages you to look into the worst case scenario to stimulate creative options and to increase your range of preparations. Remember, Walt Disney started in the Great Depression. Just as in Darwinian biology, 'survival of the fittest' will be the governing principle in the forthcoming period; the businesses that fit best to the new context will survive in preference to those that do not.

In order to rapidly adapt and to ensure your business does not succumb to 'continuity bias' (the belief that things that were happening before will happen again), leaders need to cultivate a mindset that focuses on "What's new/changed?" rather than a "What will be the same?". You need to develop a theory of the market ahead for each of the three recovery scenarios outlined above. You need to explore some or all of the following dimensions:

- Changes in customers – segments, needs and priorities
- Affordability
- Channel for delivering value
- Competitor strengths, weaknesses and possible actions
- Funding availability
- Fixed and variable input costs

## Example: Co-working spaces

Co-working spaces have thrived recently as companies like We

Work have rode the back of an entrepreneurial wave. But this pandemic is a threat to any non-secured premises-based business. If lockdown persists for many months or is repeated intermittently, existing tenants may ditch their month-to-month licenses. Longer term, start ups and early stage companies may be hesitant to take on space. Here is a very brief worked example of how using the three recovery scenarios might prompt a different response:

## Scenario 1: V Shaped Bounce

The business will survive the emergency with some outstanding rents and some bad debts from which it will slowly recover. Some cost engineering will mitigate the effects. The emergency period may have revealed opportunities to help companies who need to reduce premises costs. Businesses that were negotiating leases may back out and may have need of alternative solutions. A wave of start-ups in the months or years ahead occur to take the place of larger established businesses who go out of business. Competitors who were carrying debt may not survive the recovery period offering take-over opportunities.

## Scenario 2: Hockey Stick

Bad debts, lower occupancy, home based rather than premises-based start up businesses prevail. Efforts to support existing tenants to maintain their tenancies through some deferrals of accrued debt. Cost engineering enables profitability to be achieved at a lower occupancy rate. Target larger businesses who are downshifting - shedding permanent offices and embracing online working are targets for flexible, dedicated hot-desk hubs.

## Scenario 3: Victorian Bath

Bad debts, little new business, lower prices and lower occupancy levels challenge solvency. Opportunities to innovate such as creating a public-sector funded scheme to house team start-ups as part of the recovery strategy. Shift emphasis from provision of space to incubation of businesses. Find investors who are willing and able to fund start-ups and early stage businesses to use the co-location space in return for equity shares in those businesses. Partner with Private Equity and Venture Capital companies to provide good value space to investees.

As we can see, there are possibilities in all scenarios. Even looking into the abyss can enable you to generate valuable creative ideas that could be applied under all scenarios.

Obvious short term adaptations are already occurring. Restaurants become delivery operations, personal trainers provide online classes even art galleries are offering virtual tours. For most businesses, the obvious adaptation is how your value is delivered and this will mostly be from face to face to 'live-online' or from shop premises to 'direct to your door'. How can you present this transition as a benefit? How can you mobilise operations and people to adapt as if this were your prime business? How can you make a virtue out of a necessity?

Most businesses, if they were honest, have failed to exploit the opportunities of digital because their fortunes were rooted in bricks and mortar. Even before this happened, Arcadia – owner of high street clothing stores Topshop and Dorothy Perkins had been completely outplayed online by companies such as ASOS and BooHoo. Even before lockdown and especially since, the former is struggling to survive whilst the latter are reporting booming sales. If you are a location dependent business, use this opportunity to accelerate your online capability and presence. Become location agnostic. Integrate your online and offline operations and marketing. Use this emergency period to accelerate change and don't just see it as a temporary measure. Make it part of your new normal.

### What Opportunities Lie In The New Competitive Landscape?

The emergency period is a shock to the system and governments, where they are able, have been propping up economies with generous grants, wage subsidies and loan packages. But it is the recovery period where the competitive landscape will start to change as creditors need to be paid and the support dries up. Businesses carrying heavy debt will need to find a way to restructure to satisfy desperate creditors and insolvencies will rise. Look around at your competitors. There may be valuable individuals, valuable customers, valuable products that you could consolidate into your business. Or maybe your business is not viable alone but put together with others could have a strong competitive chance. I recall speaking with the founder of four £100m+ businesses that he created using exactly this strategy. In the recession of the early 80s, he deliberately picked up failing local recruitment agencies for very little and built a market leading network to emerge from the recession.

Be vigilant and aware of the opportunties. If you are a capable purchaser, make yourself known to specialist business transfer agencies in your sector, to specialist accountants and also to your fellow MDs and CEOs.

Be kind. This is not a time for predation but it is a time when you can help to preserve good people, good products, good customer relationships and perhaps in a win-win way. If you can help a competitor to retrieve value from their failing business by joining forces, you may actually be creating a better outcome for all.

## Long term innovation

When surveyed about the financial crash of 2008-10 in 2014, surviving businesses cited innovation as the most important recovery strategy. Looking longer-term under each scenario (V, hockey stick, Victorian bath), what are the innovation opportunities? What often stops innovation is lack of time. So if your trading is severely curtailed, how can you use the time to prepare to get back into the market stronger than ever before? One software company I know, experiencing a 60% reduction in workload from suspended projects, has decided that they will use this hiatus to build a market-leading platform. Something they have dreamt of doing but never had the time to do before. It has led to talks with two significant private equity investors.

How you lead the strategic thinking in your business now will set you up for years to come. Minimise or ignore the threats and you could be vulnerable. Mitigating downside risks whilst seizing valuable opportunities could position your business to thrive in the upturn. By working with your team to provide strategic as well as emotional leadership, you can chart a course out of this situation towards recovery, renewal and reinvention.

## References

- Innovators and exporters lead the recovery / DNA of an Entrepreneur Hiscox, September 02, 2015. https://www.hiscox.co.uk/business-blog/innovators-and-exporters-lead-the-recovery-dna-of-an-entrepreneur/

## About Jim McLaughlin

Jim McLaughlin is Managing Director of Meeting Facilitators Ltd *(www.facilitator.co.uk)* and a Non Executive Director of high growth businesses in the wholesale bakery and software sectors. He runs creative meetings to enable organisations to develop and execute business strategy and performance improvement programmes in the UK and internationally.

He is frequently used by Venture Capital and Private Equity companies to assist investees to create and implement growth plans. Jim brings experience in sales, marketing, product and service innovation, teams and management. Clients include global tech companies, world leading consulting engineers, software companies and the Young Innovators programme, which he facilitated across the UK.

He recently gained distinction in Oxford University's Masters level qualification in Strategy and Innovation. He lives in London with his wife and daughters and enjoys golf, cycling and all the things the lockdown has temporarily stopped. He is learning to tolerate DIY and mowing the lawn.

*http://www.facilitator.co.uk/*

*https://www.linkedin.com/in/jimoptima/*

# Staying Resilient Right Now

## Kylie Denton

The pandemic has been like watching the longest domino line in the world spiral out of control. One simple event setting off a chain of events throughout the world in a matter of months.

Our whole world has been turned upside down and is threatening lives and livelihoods across the world. In as little as three months over a million people and 180 countries have fallen sick from this viral illness. The decisions the world leaders make for their country determines if people live or die and that is one heavy weight to carry on anyone's shoulders.

Leaders are facing an unprecedented test on their ability to lead through a crisis. Some will cripple with fear and inaction and others will move into overdrive and will be remembered as a great leader long after this crisis.

This pandemic has hit both our health and our economy and requires business leaders to have a multi-pronged response. Leaders might be asking themselves right now how resilient their business is, but I suggest we all start with a more important question and that is "how resilient are your people?"

As a business and leadership coach, every day, I am speaking to leaders, peers and professionals about the impact on peoples mental, physical and emotional health. Emotions are heightened, people are facing fear, uncertainty, sadness. Feelings of being out of control, frustration, unpredictable, irritated, unsupported and guilt just to name a few.

You will be happy to know this is all normal and certainly expected with a crisis of this scale. In times like this people look to leaders for guidance and reassurance. How you as a leader lead through this will determine your success and the success of the people around you.

I want to share with you the eight distinct qualities that will help you lead through this crisis successfully.

1. **Calm.** We all know the feeling calm people have on us so remaining as calm as possible in front of your staff and customers is important. Even if you are scared and concerned on the inside. Your staff and customers are looking for you to lead them through this difficult and uncertain time. They are watching everything you say and do. How can you project a calmer demeanour during this time?

2. **Confidence.** We know this is an important trait for any leader generally, but right now it is critical. Confident but realistic. Displaying excessive confidence despite obvious difficult conditions will lose credibility. Therefore, projecting confidence that the organisation will find its way through this whilst also showing there is uncertainty will help. How are you currently projecting your confidence?

3. **Collaboration.**Collaboration is key for any leader however during a crisis it is important you don't stick your head in the sand and make all the decisions yourself. You don't have all the answers, and no one expects you to either. Call on your team members, you peers, your mentors and speak to trusted advisers. Engaging your team will allow them to feel like they have some control over the direction of the business. Who should you be collaborating with and how will you go about it?

4. **Decisiveness.** You might be thinking "how do we even make a decision when there are so many unknowns?". One area I work with leaders on, is to look at the decisions they can make and then park the decisions they can't. When we start to look at things we have control over it allows us to gain more focus and feel more in control. Your people are looking for decisions, but they also understand there is a large element of unknown. Explain to them what we can make decisions on now and what we will make decisions on as further information comes to hand.

Write a list of decisions you can make and a list of decisions you can't make. Share this with your people.

5. **Focus.** Currently our world is full of distractions - everywhere. And it takes a real effort to stay committed and focussed. One-way you can do this, is to plan your day or week to ensure they are getting the critical and important work completed. It is so easy to become distracted and to fall into old habits of doing the work that is easy rather than the work you should be doing. How can you set up each day to focus on the top three things that are critical and important right now?

6. **Positive mindset.** This can be tough when we are all impacted so deeply. I am seeing leaders making a conscious effort to look at the positive aspects of their life and business and practice gratitude and then helping their people to do the same. Marcus Aurelius has a famous quote, *The happiness of your life depends on the quality of your thoughts.* There are many benefits to staying positive during uncertainty. What we do have control over is our mindset. How can you practise gratitude and a positive mindset?

7. **Belief.** Believe in yourself. Right now, the global pandemic has turned our world upside down and inside out. If there is ever a time to believe in yourself, it is right now. Don't wait for things to change. Lean in now, believe you can do this and turn those beliefs into self-fulfilling prophecies. Don't let fear cripple you into self-doubt and inaction. Get clear on your focus, believe in yourself and don't give up.

8. **Empathy and understanding.** Deal with the human element first. It's important that leaders demonstrate empathy and understanding that there are both personal and professional challenges that each of their people are facing during a crisis. We shouldn't just assign this to human resources and communications and feel we have done our part. We need to get in there and shows these qualities ourselves. Although it is important, we show these qualities to our people, we also need to open ourselves up to receive empathy from others and to remain attentive to our own wellbeing. Stress, fatigue and uncertainty limits our ability to process information, remain level-headed and to exercise good judgement. Investing time in your own well being will allow you to sustain your effectiveness over the weeks and months to come. What are some ways that

you will show empathy and understanding to your people and to yourself?

Although these qualities are important, we must remember that what wraps around these qualities is the human element. Each one of us, is in some way affected by this pandemic, but how it is affecting us is different.

Although we are all experiencing similar emotions our situations are different and unique to each one of us. People are now having to work from home, working out of bedrooms, lounge rooms, and back gardens, noise all around them, young kids screaming and school kids that are now doing schooling online, are bored and miss their friends. So many distractions to deal with yet all so unique to the individual.

I hosted a webinar recently where we had a guy sitting on his bed in his 2-bedroom unit, with his newborn and wife in another room. This was his new office for 8 hours a day. Others are separated from loved ones, some are sick, some are living in small spaces with no spare rooms for offices, others have so many people in the house it is hard to work let alone think with any substance.

For anyone managing people, this new world requires more than just the impacts on the business it means managing people's emotions, keeping them focused, agile and managing change rapidly and in adverse situations.

We must put people first if we want our business to survive or dare I say it thrive. We need to support our people. We need to be able to understand their own situation.

Here are some example questions that you can use with your people to understand their own situation and how you can help them.

- How are you managing and coping?

- What does your home life look like right now?

- Do you have a dedicated space to work in?

- Who else is at home? How is that impacting on you?

- What is challenging you right now?

- What do I need to know about you right now?

- How is your work impacted?

- What can I do to help?

Make a positive difference in people's lives. Doing this requires leaders to acknowledge the personal and professional challenges that employees and their loved ones are experiencing and by asking these questions will allow you to get closer to their true situation and challenges they are facing.

Everyone will need you differently and until you know how you can help them you won't be able to help them enough.

The most important point to remember is that we are all feeling right now. We are all trying to put on a brave face and make sense of what this new world looks like but deep down we are all a little heavy and a little out of sorts and processing it in the best way we can. So give each other a lot of grave, be kind but be clear and help where each one of your people need as best as you can and don't forget to also give some to yourself because all of this is new to you too.

Don't wait for things to change, lean in now become the leader you always dreamed of. This is your time to shine, believe in yourself and lead your troops to victory.

## About Kylie Denton

Kylie Denton is a bestselling author and highly experienced business consultant, professionally certified coach and speaker specialising in the financial services, banking, insurance and wealth management industries.

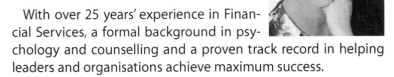

With over 25 years' experience in Financial Services, a formal background in psychology and counselling and a proven track record in helping leaders and organisations achieve maximum success.

Kylie Denton is a professionally qualified Organisational and Leadership Coach, experienced in leadership coaching, executive coaching and team coaching. Kylie works with companies to help them improve productivity and performance and develop current, emerging and future leaders both personally and professionally.

Kylie has this innate ability to truly connect and understand her client's and is known for her ability to take people and organisations to the next level and turn good leaders into great leaders. Kylie pushes her coaching clients out of their comfort zone and challenges them to be the change they want to see in themselves and their business.

Kylie always has a wealth of information to share so reach out and connect

*Kylie@performanceadvisorygroup.com.au*

*https://performanceadvisorygroup.com.au/*

*https://www.linkedin.com/in/kyliedenton5/*

*https://twitter.com/kyliedenton5*

*https://www.instagram.com/performanceadvisorygroup/*

*https://www.linkedin.com/in/kyliedenton5/*

# Governing In A Crisis

## Dr Karl George MBE

Hindsight is a wonderful thing for telling us what we COULD have done when we were in the middle of a crisis. But what do we, as business leaders, do right NOW during the pandemic to ensure that our businesses survive? Surrounded by uncertainty, how do we plan for the future and decide on what to do next?

I always try to look through the governance lens when searching for answers. I don't want knee-jerk reactions. I look for answers that consider both the short-term and long-term implications and provide a real sense of direction and leader-ship.

I mentioned that hindsight is a great teacher. So, what did we learn after the Walker Review following the 2008 banking crisis; the inquiry findings after the 2017 Grenfell tragedy; the findings of the White House commission following the BP oil spill in 2010; the Laming inquiry into the tragic death of Victoria Climbie in 2000 or the 2013 Francis Inquiry following apparently high mortality rates in an NHS trust?

Some damning comments from these, and other inquiries, are listed below. They make cautionary reading for leaders dealing with a major crisis.

Let's ensure we aren't accused of incompetence, complacency or negligence.

- "There were a series of almost incredible failures in the days and hours leading up to the disaster."

- "The companies involved in the disaster were operating under a 'culture of complacency' and need top-to-bottom reform."

- "The judge described the failures of statutory and other agencies as 'blinding incompetence.'"

- "This negligent financial management rendered the charity incapable of surviving any variance in its funding stream."

- "All failed to properly investigate the case and little action was

- "The trustees were 'negligent' and ignored repeated warnings about the organisation's financial health, MPs said as they outlined an 'extraordinary catalogue of failures' leading to the collapse."

Leadership guru John Maxwell defined a crisis as 'an intense time of difficulty requiring a decision that will be a turning point'.

So, now I want to share four principles that we all need during a crisis. They are the need for strong leadership; an appropriate governance structure; a cognitively diverse team and the will and capacity to make swift decisions and act on them.

## 1. Strong Leadership

The first principle is strong, flexible and visible leadership. You should ensure that your leadership is positive, forward-looking, well-informed but decisive.

Before you do anything, you need to determine the scale of the actions that need to be taken and how far-reaching they will be. Get an angle on liquidity and solvency and how resilient you are as a business. Pulling together relevant, accurate facts will be crucial.

The CEO is the chief crisis manager and communicator and the board operates in the background to provide oversight advice and support led by the Chair.

An example of strong leadership is how Martin Luther King Junior mobilised a nation when he led the African American civil rights movement in the United States. He was confronted by every obstacle imaginable but remained positive, strong and visible. His powerful communication skills are evidenced by how often his speeches and quotations are repeated more than 50 years later.

In his 1964 acceptance speech for the Nobel Peace Prize, King said that the civil rights movement, and his personal commitment to it, was grounded in optimism. He spoke of an 'abiding faith in America and an audacious faith in the future of mankind'. He said: "I refuse to accept the view that mankind is so tragically bound to the starless midnight of racism and war that the bright daybreak of peace and brotherhood can never become a reality."

Your role as a leader in a crisis is to help people get through it, to reassure them and give them the right perspective. Bad leadership just accelerates the crisis and it is unavoidable that it will be exposed.

## 2. Relevant Governance Structure

The second principle involves the governance structure and the importance of everyone having clear roles and responsibilities and understanding the boundaries. The CEO has oversight and a strategic role and should develop a core team of executives.

An example of this is the UK Government's emergency COBRA meetings. COBRA stands for Cabinet Office Briefing Room A, which is where these meetings usually take place. As well as the Prime Minister, who usually chairs the meetings, they are attended by a cross departmental range of senior ministers, security officials, military chiefs, emergency services leaders and civil servants. The attendees change according to the nature of the crisis. Medical and scientific experts have been brought in for coronavirus meetings.

Similarly, in your business or organisation you need to develop an extended team that will be brought in for specific responses. We typically ask the board, i.e. the non-executives, to stay strategic, to challenge the executive, to be ambassadors to all stakeholders and get to grips with the key risks. A crisis is the time to exercise all of those roles, but it is even more important to take a more collaborative approach than is normally expected. The board may need to dig a little bit deeper than normal when providing support and advice, but it is important to get the balance right so there is not interference. Non-executive directors may be required to join a particular 'task and finish' group and serve the organisation with their specialist skills.

### 3. Cognitively Diverse Team

To ensure that we have the right mix of skills and capabilities to address all of the challenges that are going to come about in a crisis, we need an effective team that we can leverage and use.

In his book, *Good to Great*, Jim Collins creates a memorable metaphor by comparing a business to a bus and its leader as the bus driver. He says you must always start by getting the right people on the bus, the wrong people off the bus, and the right people in the right seats.

During a crisis, you can't have hangers-on. Everyone needs to step up and be in alignment. We need to make the best use of the talent that we have, ensuring that we avoid the temptation to work only with the people with whom we are most comfortable. We don't want group-think, but neither do we want conflict. There should be healthy collaborative tension. The governance structure, mentioned in the last principle, may not have all of the current leaders operating in their normal capacity. In times of crisis there will be key individuals who step up to the plate, from different disciplines or backgrounds. It is imperative that bureaucracy, or overly-rigid governance structures, don't stop employees at all levels from being empowered to carry out their roles.

## 4. Decide and Act

It is important for a leader to be open, authentic and accountable for their decisions. They need to listen first, take everyone's views and all the facts into account and then exercise good judgement to make a firm decision and take action.

Under this principle, a good leader will stand by their decisions, however difficult they are and however unpalatable they may be to others.

Everyone is in this together and a good leader takes decisions in the knowledge that the buck stops with them.

Although I recommend that you don't react impulsively to the crisis and make kneejerk decisions without gathering information, you must also act swiftly. Decisions must be made in a structured manner once all the relevant information has been gathered.

It's impossible to know at this stage whether the UK Government's decisions on actions to reduce and prevent the spread of coronavirus took too long. Only hindsight will tell us whether they were right or wrong.

In conclusion, here are a few tips to consider as you develop your plans for leading your business or organisation out of a crisis:

- Keep a cool head and stay in charge;
- Don't burnout. Take care of yourself. It will get intense;
- Gather the right information quickly and educate yourself about the crisis;
- Ensure your business continuity plan is up to date;
- Communicate adequately with external and internal stakeholders;
- Ensure the leadership team stays on top of social media;
- Don't hide the facts but ensure you separate them from emotions, which may run high;

- Every crisis has financial implications. Put together the financial mitigation strategy;

- Don't react. Stay rational and systematic before making decisions;

- Adjust to the new reality, making sure you adjust your mental attitude;

- Be agile and swift to make adjustments once you've taken the time to analyse the new reality;

- Consult and learn from your peers;

- Be an authentic leader and practise what you preach;

- Ensure there are no surprises. Keep your board informed;

- Have empathy, sympathy and understanding for all stakeholders;

- Transparency and openness are important. Ensure you keep communicating effectively.

## About Dr Karl George MBE

Dr Karl George MBE is a thought leader, author and internationally established consultant in governance. He is Managing Director of *the governance forum (tgf)*, creator of The Governance Framework and the Effective Board Member Programmes. He works with boards and senior executives in the private, public and voluntary sectors and has over twenty five years' combined experience in accountancy, business and strategic development.

Karl is a Fellow both of the global accounting body ACCA and of international body for governance practitioners ICSA: The Chartered Governance Institute. He has developed a unique governance framework and kitemark that was endorsed by the late Sir Adrian Cadbury.

Karl is the author of the *tgf Governance Code* – principles of governance of governance for organisations of all sizes, sectors and geographical jurisdictions. His latest book, *The Effective Board Member* immediately went to number one in the Best Sellers list for Management and Leadership on Amazon Kindle.

*www.karlgeorge.com*

*Instagram - @karlgeorgembe*

*Twitter - @karlgeorgembe*

# Leading The Rebound From The Pandemic - The Next Futures Of Organizations, Work, And The Workplace

## Rohit Talwar CEO Fast Future

Will new ways of organizational thinking and working take hold or be abandoned as soon as the coronavirus lockdowns are lifted?

The pandemic has been with us for just a few months and we are just weeks into a near global lockdown. However, we're already developing insights on the emerging possible futures of business, work and the workplace. Already, many have reshaped themselves, with most employees working from home. For some, total rethinking of their strategy, business model, technology platforms, operating design, supply chain, and partnership ecosystem has been necessary. Here are ten shifts organizations are embracing that could have lasting impacts.

### 1. The New Leadership

Leaders are beginning to appreciate the importance of flexibility and experimentation - from business models and distribution systems to organization of work and management of a home-based workforce. Empathy and emotionally literate leadership are becoming critical. The crisis highlights those with the capacity to engage, motivate, and lead when all staff engagement is done via video and telephone. In video mode, we may well be missing some of the subtle cues embedded in physical interactions.

Instead, the best leaders are learning to acknowledge their fears, uncertainties, and adaptation challenges, and to ask deeper questions that allow people to share their concerns and needs in a rapidly changing environment. With many roles under scrutiny in cost focused environments, for some in management and leadership roles, the situation is quite exposing - revealing that their jobs lacked substance or impact.

## 2. Innovation

Necessity is driving invention. Radical ideas are emerging for every challenge. At the macro level, previously unthinkable ideas are being trialled, such as guaranteed basic incomes, compulsory population health testing, total lockdowns, and border closures. Organizationally, for many, innovation has become a survival priority rather than just a budget item.

The need for ideas at speed is driving rapid experimentation – with often incredible results. For example, massive global self-organizing networks have formed to share data, algorithms, and computing resources to tackle different aspects of modelling pandemics and generating, simulating, and testing alternative medical solutions and response strategies. Similarly, essential medical equipment prototypes are being designed and 3D printed in days rather than months or years.

The innovation process is also being reimagined. Pre-crisis, we'd witnessed continual growth in different facilitated innovation approaches. This is now being embraced in the virtual space. The need for variety in online meeting experiences is driving organizations to trial a variety of accelerated innovation approaches from sprints to crowdsourcing.

## 3. Culture, Empowerment, and Trust

Major cultural challenges are emerging for predominantly office-based organizations where physical environments helped shape and reinforce culture. They are learning to introduce virtual mechanisms to replace informal chats, fly by conversations, serendipitous water cooler encounters, and lunch and learn sessions. With most organizations still bedding down new ways of working and trying to embrace uncertainty and volatility, management is often highly preoccupied with the now, the near, and the next. Rapid waves of redundancies are flattening some management structures and increasing responsibility spans.

These changes and the speed at which events are unfolding drive greater delegation of authority, enabling individuals to respond to rapidly changing realities. Allowing staff to take more responsibility, show more initiative, and make more decisions should highlight the extent to which greater trust can be invested in the workforce. The changes will also highlight where trust needs to be backed with training, coaching, and review as people learn to operate with less supervision and instruction.

### 4. Prioritisation and Decision Making

The sheer scale of change and differing levels of impact are driving organizations to get smarter about project and task prioritization. Many are challenging the near- and medium-term value of every initiative and evaluating their chances of success under different post-pandemic scenarios. Focusing on the vital few is freeing up time and allowing potential acceleration of pivot projects that respond to the changing opportunity landscape. In many cases, large digital transformation projects are being suspended, with emphasis and resources shifting to truly transformational opportunities that could prove more fruitful in the new economy, using technologies such as artificial intelligence.

With meetings moving online, willingness to experiment with more participatory collaborative decision-making approaches is growing. The simple act of a moderator controlling who speaks in group chats changes discussions, people can finish their points without interruption, and everyone's voice can be heard. The loudest voices need not dominate. The crisis is also driving willingness to experiment with crowd sourcing, collective intelligence, and group decision making tools that offer engaging ways of getting to decisions, appreciating differing perspectives, and reaching buy-in or consensus.

## 5. Learning

The situation is driving learning at every level. This starts from basic adaptation challenges such as how to work productively while your children are across the room doing homework or playing. The need to use remote working tools is forcing people to acquire greater technology awareness. At a broader level, there is a strong imperative to raise our scientific literacy to understand concepts such as the basics of the coronavirus, exponential growth, and the science behind social distancing.

At the macro level, leaders and employees alike are having to learn about notions like scenario thinking to prepare for a range of possible futures - from scenarios for pandemic evolution over the coming months to different possible economic outlooks for markets, nations, and the planet. Cutting commuting time also provides time to learn new skills from mastering meditation and flower arranging to data science, artificial intelligence, and behavioural economics – online course enrolment is rising. The benefits of a constantly learning workforce could become evident across many aspects of what organizations do in future – from strategic thinking through to experimenting with new technologies and approaches.

## 6. Digital Literacy

By the end of the crisis we could see a more digitally capable workforce – with massive benefits when delivering technology change programmes. Many are investing the time saved on commuting to deepen digital literacy – from learning productivity functions in Word and PowerPoint to taking online classes in technologies that could form part of their next task or job.

## 7. Productivity and Efficiency

Many report that productivity and efficiency are improving through reduced workplace interruptions, project cancellations, and greater attention on clear communications. Individuals can focus more effectively on core tasks and learn productivity enhancing skills. Research on telecommuting has consistently suggested that remote workers are more productive than office-based counterparts. The pandemic may be a significant tipping point in the work-from-home trend if many companies decide employees should remain remote.

## 8. Flexibility and Adaptability

Organisationally, firms are adapting both what they do and how they do it - at speed. For example, convention centres being repurposed as hospitals, restaurants pivoting to cater for essential workers and takeaway delivery, and event organisers repositioning exhibitions and conferences as online offerings and community building activities.

Others, such as grounded airlines, are having to face the challenge of laying off large numbers of flight crews or repurposing them. New tasks include critical service innovations, supporting healthcare professionals in non-clinical roles, and training that will help differentiate brands when the recovery starts.

Managers and workers are having to find workarounds of how to do things they previously took for granted or never had to worry about. Organizations are constantly changing priorities, reshaping, cutting headcounts, and freezing hiring.

In response, individuals are having to take on new roles, tasks, and responsibilities at speed and learn to develop rapport with others who they may not previously have encountered or managed.

This is driving the demand for training in collaboration, cultural awareness, flexibility, adaptability, coping with chaos, and decision making under uncertainty.

## 9. Collaboration and Ecosystems

New partnerships and collaborations are becoming commonplace – as evidenced by the unusual alliances forming between Formula One race teams and aviation equipment manufacturers to design and develop ventilators. How many other real-world challenges could these new ecosystems be harnessed to address?

Governments are working with the public, voluntary, and private sector to address challenges on a previously unseen and unimaginable scale. For example, over 750,000 people volunteered to support the UK National Health Service and wider society – in everything from transporting patients to delivering food to people in self-quarantine and calling those in isolation. Similarly, a range of resources and facilities have been mobilised to take all of the homeless off the streets within days – something that was previously considered a five to ten-year challenge. Again, the question arises as to how many of these new solutions and ways and mobilising resources at scale could become part of the fabric of civil society going forward?

## 10. Foresight, Scenario Thinking, and Resilience

For many, the crisis has highlighted the need to be better prepared for the unexpected as well as our "assumed or preferred future". This is driving demand for skills in horizon scanning for future risks and opportunities. From being a "nice to have", scenario planning is becoming a critical tool to explore different possible ways in which developments might combine and play out in the coming weeks, months, and years.

Some are also learning to use these future insights and scenarios to expand the range and severity of risk impacts factored into their resilience and recovery plans. For many, there is also a growing recognition, at national and entity level, that well thought through and properly tested contingency plans, supporting resources, and mobilization protocols have to be in place to respond quickly, effectively, and assuredly to avoid having to make too many decisions from scratch in the middle of an unfolding crisis.

The situation has presented organizations with a "not to be wasted" opportunity to acquire new approaches, ways of thinking, and skills that can help navigate the current crisis and lay the foundations for the next future of work.

## Questions

1. How is the balance of conversation and focus shifting in your organization between addressing immediate operational challenges and thinking about future scenarios, strategies, and the organization of work?

2. How are you and your organization managing the mental health risks associated with the lack of work-based social interaction through the switch to home working?

3. What approaches – skills, tools, coaching support – are you and your organization deploying to maximise productivity?

4. Which changes that you see being implemented now to ensure operational continuity do you expect to remain in place post-pandemic?

## About Rohit Talwar CEO Fast Future

Rohit Talwar is a global futurist, strategic adviser, entrepreneur, and the CEO of Fast Future. Through his speaking, executive education, research, consultancy, and publishing he advises leaders in global businesses, government, and NGOs around the world on how to anticipate and respond to disruptive change. Rohit is currently advising on how to respond to the COVID-19 disruption, prepare for a range of possible future scenarios, and develop greater resilience and anticipatory capabilities in our lives, our organizations, and our countries. He has spoken to leadership audiences in over 70 countries on six continents.

Rohit has co-written and edited seven books on the emerging future and how to navigate it. His forthcoming book *Aftershocks and Opportunities – Scenarios for a Post-Pandemic Future* draws on contributions from thought leaders around the world to explore the emerging possibilities and risks and the resulting critical actions required to navigate our way out of the current health crisis and economic disruption,

*rohit@fastfuture.com*

*Mob +44 (0)7973 405145*

*www.fastfuture.com*

*LinkedIn: https://www.linkedin.com/in/rohit-talwar-futurist-keynote-speaker/*

*Twitter: @fastfuture*

*Facebook: https://www.facebook.com/RohitKTalwar*

# To Lead Others, You Must Lead Yourself

**Lucy Barkas**

If there was ever a test to what kind of leader you are, lead during a crisis. Believe me I have met some brilliant leaders who are great a building things but get bored when it's built. Even Sir Winston Churchill struggled to adapt to peacetime leadership. For today's modern leader, leading through uncertainty is now the normal landscape. The leader who passes the test is flexible, adaptable, cool under pressure and leads hearts and minds towards a purpose and a vision. The 2020's will be the decade of rapid global change, assembling matrix/tactical and diverse teams and we need a new generation of leaders.

Let's start off with a little context. Whether it's a flood, fires, stock market crashes, or an M&A, sudden change is inevitable. When it happens, we all jump into crisis management instantly. There is huge energy and adrenaline as everyone busies themselves in survival mode and adrenaline is pumping through our veins, giving razor sharp focus under pressure. Soon that initial hiatus of action shifts towards a new rhythm and everyone begins to adjust. We seek reassurance from our leaders, so we feel that we are in safe hands. We seek stability in an out-of-control world, and a consistent leadership approach will do that, and we look for a plan to follow, even if it's just until the end of the week or month.

Being the leader can be exhausting if you try to do it alone. Many do not recognise the emotional, mental and physical stress that any huge change has on them. You will be experiencing similar fears, concerns and anxiety as everyone else – you are human after all. And when your people look to you for all the answers, even though you have few, you might feel the enormous pressure or responsibility of leadership. I want you to know this is normal, and you don't have to do it alone. I will share some tips and approaches which will accelerate you through the change process and be the leader your people need and deserve.

In any change process I use my *5My's Method*.

## MyPresent

The *MyPresent* step is focusing on right now, your current state – and I just want you to focus on you as a human being. Notice your thoughts, feelings and how your body is feeling and how you are behaving. You are gathering information about where you are on the change journey and how it is impacting your leadership. Are you still high alert, super vigilant and reacting? Are you always on, waking at 4 am with your mind racing? Perhaps you have transitioned through to the cortisol come down that hits you like a bolt out of the blue. You may feel exhausted, unable to concentrate for long periods or your memory might be fuzzy. Or perhaps you feel like you are coming out of the other side and logic and reasoning, even creativity and strategic thinking are returning, and you are energised. Notice – where are you right now, and how is it impacting your ability to lead?

*"Before you assist others, always put your oxygen mask on first."*

Take the time to recharge your batteries, calm your mind and be the best that you can be for your people. And when you are aware of where you are in the change cycle, you can easily spot where others are, and be there for them in the right way.

First comes denial. The mind is in shock and can't make sense of the world, so it freezes. You may hear yourself saying that *It's not that bad, It won't amount to anything, It won't impact me.* Then your brain starts to process that this change is happening, and it starts freaking out a little. You might become anxious, overwhelmed or depressed or go into doing mode, or need to withdraw and disengage. You will get angry, short tempered or make snap judgements about others. These are all normal reactions to a threat. Just notice and process it. We need you to move through it so you can lead consciously and make great decisions.

Eventually your brain needs to make sense of everything, so you seek information, validation and root causes. This could turn into finger pointing or blame, or spending hours in social media or the news. Your brain trying to make sense of the world, finding some order in the chaos. Notice when you are here and how it might be influencing your decisions or behaviours. You may become frustrated with others who are dancing around emotion, or dismissive of other views that challenge yours. As the leader, you must self-regulate quickly and not shoot from the hip.

And soon you are ready to accept your reality. I find for many clients, this stage comes as a sigh of relief, like the calm skies after a storm. It is tempting to stay here a little and smell the new fresh air – soak it up and simply be but it won't last for long.

Your brain will soon push you to "change", which shows up as new energy or an explosion of ideas. You can clearly see the road ahead and become excited about the possibilities. You are in a state of renewal and optimism.

So simply check in on yourself and notice where you are right now, be kind to yourself, and be with that for a while – then talk to people about where you are now. Talking really helps, and when you can be vulnerable with your trusted team, it further strengthens the bonds between you. If you don't have that kind of team, then building one might be the most urgent priority for you when you are in the change mindset. You can't do this alone.

## Myself

Now you know where you are, you can focus on who you need to be. In times of stress we tend to overplay our strengths, which can be a blessing and a curse. Knowing what these are is essential so that you can use them consciously and know when to dial them up or down. Some people are very naturally risk takers, adventurous and results driven, others are more creative, blue skies thinkers who love spontaneity and human contact. Both are great when you want to get into action and move things forward, but what if your people are stuck in emotion or justification mode? They really don't need your energy right now. They need your understanding and empathy. You might be the supportive kind of leader who listens, comforts and seeks to please, but what if your people are done processing and need direction and a plan? Knowing yourself and how you are behaving means that you can consciously adapt to the needs of your people. Mastering emotional intelligence is what will really give you the leadership edge.

Here are some tips I have been sharing with my clients over recent weeks to ground them and help them to be the best they can be right now.

1. Focus on three key priorities at any one time. Sure, you have a million things to be doing, but you realistically can't give 100% focus to that many. Decide what 3 things each day are deal breakers and do them. If you have time of course you can do more, but don't overload yourself – then communicate those three priorities with the team.

2. Slow down. In those early days of change you were running full steam ahead. Now is the time to slow down and take stock. Create some thinking space for yourself to simply ponder. In doing so, you calm your mind and become so much clearer on what needs to be done and how.

3. Reflect. What has gone well? What hasn't? How did you show up today and did it work? Were you the best you could be that day and what have you learned as a result? This is all valuable information you will need later.

4. Talk to people. If you haven't got a trusted group around you, colleagues who you really trust, then find someone. It could be an old friend, a mentor or a coach, but find someone who can help you explore what's is going on, declutter your mind and help you move forward with clarity.

5. Be kind to yourself. Look, you have never been in this exact situation before and might make a few mistakes along the way. Forgive yourself and make the intention to do better next time.

6. Try and reconnect with your purpose. You became a leader for a reason – what was it? Why this business? Why this industry? What is the impact that you want to make? Once you reconnect with that, you find your direction and clarity.

7. Get physical. Move, stretch, go for a walk or take some exercise. Moving your body really does reset your mind and give you a new perspective. A cluttered mind can become still by simply moving.

And now you are ready to lead your team consciously and with purpose.

## About Lucy Barkas

Lucy Barkas, Founder of 3WH, a leadership and team development consultancy has been in the leadership field for over 20 years. She is the author of LeaderX, and the host of the LeaderX podcast as well as a regular contributor on BBC Radio.

She helps leaders to create strong, unified leadership teams who in turn lead the organisation tow achieve its purpose and vision – using the *5 MYs* methodology.

*www.3wh.uk.com*

*https://www.linkedin.com/in/lucybarkas/*

*https://www.facebook.com/3WHLeadership/*

# Winning At Home And In Business

## Jonnie Jensen

Turning round to find that your family checked out long before is no victory. Success is winning the game in business and at home.

We may be in a unique time but as we juggle business with homeschooling the challenges are just an exaggerated version of the ones we face all the time.

The journey with your family - seeing them grow as you and your business does - is part of the experience of being a modern business leader. To lose that is a pain best avoided.

It's as much a commitment as it is a state of mind. Making sure your team at home is as important to you as your team at work.

For some, it is the practical balance of time and not being able to be in two places at once. For others, it is harder to shift between "Boss hat" and "Dad hat". Relationships quickly suffer either way.

Some end up feeling guilty about it. Others are resentful that their family is not grateful for how hard they work. Neither are helpful and not something to get stuck in.

Success at work. Happiness at home. The business leader that has this can wake up positive and go to bed satisfied.

Of course, there are sacrifices to be made as you grow a successful business but when those around you are "in on the deal" then you stand a better chance of them sticking with you. They want to feel inspired by you, not sidelined.

Just as in work, leadership at home takes planning, communication and reward.

I'm not telling you how to parent. I have taken what I've learnt and I apply it to my family. It works for us…. most of the time!. It is an ongoing endeavour.

## Under The Microscope Everything Looks Big

In these upside down times of a global pandemic, business leaders are being forced to confront change like none of us has ever done before. Plus they have do it whilst being a home-school teacher and spending 24hrs a day with their partner.

Of course it feels stressful!

Some will struggle that is for sure. Some will thrive. One person's frustration at being a full-time parent is another's delight as they finally get to be at home more and enjoy their children. As a divorced parent who only sees his children 50% of the time I've had to learn the tough way.

Make the most of this time - anytime - with your family. Before you know it they will be grown up.

Like any project bring some structure. Get really organised with workspace and schedule the day. It won't be much different from their school day but you may need to share it with your staff. If both parents are at home focus on your strengths and weaknesses. If neither of you can do Physics get creative. Could another parent that is help via a video call?

Make it work. Set times for breaks and have lunch together. Segment work and family time and do not let them overlap. You'll be more effective in both.

Don't get frustrated and angry. If you have back to back meetings in the office you just get on with it and work late. Perhaps this is a time to become more accepting at home also.

Make time to play and do not sweat the small stuff. If you have more than one child then try to give each some quality time. Spend 30 minutes with your children playing football in the garden or making Tik Tock videos together. And then afterwards when they have been on their phone or Xbox too long, let it go. If it means they are interacting with their friends and you can work without distraction, then it's a WIN WIN.

## Become A Family That Speaks To Each Other

There can't be many authoritarian top-down business leaders still. Well, Donald Trump aside! Strangely though it still seems quite common in peoples homes and that doesn't mean it's always the man. From the amount I hear of people being bossed around or ignored by their partner, it is a problem. When you add on top of that challenges of managing teenagers then you have a clear communication breakdown.

Not so in the workplace. Here we are used to regular communication, with idea sharing, delegation and agreements. It is unlikely that families speak of conversations in those same terms but regardless it's a good way to operate.

Conversation with your partner is vital. Be interested in each other. If you find that hard then it is likely you are not spending quality time together. People often talk about having a 'date night' with your partner and of course that makes sense. By the time my ex-wife and I started doing it though so much resentment had set in that even that became something to argue about. The solution to this is to clear out those resentments each week so they do not build up.

- "Is there anything this week that I could have done for you that I didn't?"

- "Was there anything this week that I said I would do for you that I did not do?"

- "Is there anything I could do differently next week that would work better for you?"

Questions like these will allow a reset and for you both to feel fully supported.

Regular conversation with our children is immensely rewarding. I make time each day to ask my children how their day went. *What were the best bits of your day?* This naturally opens them up to talking. It is easy enough to then ask *Did anything go wrong that I can help with?* And to finish with *What do you want tomorrow to look like?*

If you and your children are not used to talking then it may not go well to start with but this is a good open structure. Of course, it can be tricky with teenagers but the more you bring conversation into your relationship then the easier it becomes.

Bizarrely so few families make the time to plan. Bizarre because at work we seem to spend half our day in meetings. Set up weekly meetings at home and plan ahead. You'll be amazed at how much smoother life becomes.

Plan five weeks ahead. You'll know what is on the horizon and can decide who is going to take care of it. Of course plan ahead for the bigger events - birthdays, Christmas, summer holiday - and you can also include things you want to do but are unlikely. They'll be even more unlikely if you never talk about them.

By involving your children they'll be more agreeable to the plans and you'll teach them an incredible lesson for living a successful life.

## Become A Team With Your Family

It is powerful to instil a sense of team in your family. When you think about sports teams they have shared goals and a vision for their future. Play well, win trophies. It pulls them together. It creates direction and routines fall into place. In times of uncertainty, such foundations become something you can all count on.

Get connected with your family around a vision for the future. For couples, it's quite normal in the early days but it gets lost under the rigour of daily life. Play with your plans for the future. It is all made up anyway. Imagine living in Ibiza and running a bar. Probably ridiculous but it may have you see you would like to live near the sea and be around more people.

For children, outrageous goals for the future are generally easier. What they are more concerned about is their day to day lives. This for them is the consistency they rely on. Watching their favourite TV show, seeing Grandparents, playing for their football team, dancing in the upcoming show. When you are a child - even a teenager - time moves so much slower and hence these are what's important.

Make sure you know what is important to them. Find out what they are worried about. You may be pulling your hair out about them not doing a piece of school work, when the answer lies in a concern they have about something completely different.

You can then manage and adjust what is important to them. If it is your team at work it's the coffee, bonuses and time off. Of course they do not share your stresses but that is why you are the boss. Your family need reassuring just as your staff do.

Make the normal awesome. Laugh as often as possible. Trust each other. Say "Yes" more than you say *No*. Watch a regular TV program or play a family computer game together. Get outside. And more than anything acknowledge them.

At work that is saying *Thank you* and giving them Friday afternoon off. In your family that is saying *I love you* and treating them to something they enjoy - you might just find that is spending quality time with you.

## About Jonnie Jensen

Jonnie Jensen is the founder of *TeamSuperDad.com* which is an online community, podcast and training pro-gramme for Dads that want to be more, earn more and play more. Having previ-ously been a Digital Marketing Consultant with 20 years in the industry, Jonnie was inspired to create Team Super Dad after his marriage breakdown and the challenges he experienced rebuilding his life.

He is a father, son and brother with two children, Jago and Rosie, plus step-son Archie. As well as a passion for fitness and well-being Jonnie is a certified Firewalking instructor. You can find him by his name or *Team Super Dad* on most social channels:

*@JonnieJensen*

*linkedin.com/in/jonniejensen*

*teamsuperdad.com*

*facebook.com/teamsuperdad*

*Team Super Dad Podcast @ podfollow.com/1483616441*

# Needed-Now Leadership

## Andrew Priestley

I am very privileged to be the Chairman of *Clear Sky Children's Charity* (UK). We provide play therapy for children aged 4 to 12 who have witnessed or directly experienced a trauma. Based on the Theory of Attachment, play therapy, under carefully orchestrated and monitored and safeguarded conditions, works wonders. Clearly, a child can not engage in talking therapy but I am constantly inspired to hear that children have been able to process some profound complex adult emotions via play therapy.

In some cases, they get their childhood back. And childhood is precious. Especially now. We have seen the biggest recorded spike in domestic violence in the UK - ever. For example, I recently saw report of nine coronavirus deaths … and nine women dead from domestic violence.

Think about that. Kids are on the front line.

It's been a hectic two months for us. For the executive and the Trustees. We normally meet every quarter - but recently we have been meeting weekly such is the rate of changes that need responding to.

When the government started locking down the UK in late March - shutting schools - our play therapists were deemed essential workers. We sought advice from the Government, the NHS and the various Play Therapist professional bodies on how to handle this compliantly. Even after the Easter holiday term break began parents were still sending children to school! For example, we had a case where one little five year old turned up in pyjama top and shorts and slippers and as little as a week ago, early April it was still chilly mornings. A vulnerable child.

Fortunately, one of our play therapists was there.

Now they don't have to be. They are deemed essential but it is entirely up to their discretion as to whether they are on call or not. We cannot ask someone to endanger their own health.

What makes frustrating is the parents who believe they can and should be able to avail themselves of community services. What drives it is a sense of entitlement or straight up ignorance. To be fair, in a lot of cases, the parents are known. They have issues themselves - and sending a child to school is their solution.

It challenges me on many levels. I am an ex-school teacher and I once taught in a remote country school and I have seen a lot of stuff that makes you frustrated, angry … or weep.

But as a charity, we are purposed to respond despite our judgements and disbelief.

Our challenge from a leadership perspective has been to keep the services of the charity running throughout this period. It is not easy.

We have had to furlough staff - so whatever we are doing is being done - nationally - on a skeleton crew. The executive team took most of our programs online rapidly and so we have been making much needed free and low cost resources available to teachers, parents and therapists.

What I am noticing is that the team are leading where they stand. It is very much a co-lead charity at the moment.

As Trustees our job is to support the executive team and to ensure that everything we do is transparent and passes the scrutiny the Charities Commission. Juggling compliance with empathy has been an experience in itself but what inspires me is just how focus and bonded we have become as a team working under pressure.

As Chairman I cannot give my opinion or direction - that is the role of the executive on the front line - but as the chair of Trustees I can ensure that we create a environment where the executive can  problem solve put loud.

What has stunned me is the level of grant funding that we have been able to attract recently because we kept showing up. We kept demonstrating value. To be fair, we were required to keep people in the loop, and we have been letting people - teachers, parents, therapists - know that the charity is still operable and they are supported still.

It is humbling. Truly humbling.

I am speaking for my self here but the lessons I am learning is when the need is clear you van drive efficiencies rapidly. We have been pivoting at lightning speed - failing fast for sure - but the recovery response has turned into rapid response.

Clayton Christensen in his profound book *How Will You Measure Your Life?* - Probably the best book I have ever read on the spirit of stewardship and leadership - talks about what drives people.

Basically, it is hygiene and motivation.

Hygiene is basically what's my salary, what are my working hours and conditions. Extrinsic stuff. Motivation is intrinsic. And more salient than hygiene.

I have seen team members - on furlough volunteer their time to keep Clear Sky going. They don't have to. I have seen our unpaid volunteers continue to volunteer. Why? They are not being paid. And as mentioned, the executive team and my fellow Trustees have gone above and beyond.

I mentioned it before but I feel we have drawn closer as a charity. I feel we have stepped up and I know that has not gone unnoticed.

It disheartens me to even contemplate what some of our vulnerable kids are experiencing right now. I know that requests for therapy have spiked. I am concerned that too many of those requests are because lockdown has created an environment that in some homes is unsafe and volatile.

I mentor leaders world wide. I recently had a management meeting with a large company that there minutes into the call the long knives were drawn. Finger pointing. Labelling. Bickering. I called time out!

I know this company and one of their corporate vales is respect. I called them on it. "Guys, I can't see any respect here." As a team we decided to nominate five rules of engagement. The first being was to be honest about how you are feeling. We made it OK to not have answers.

Having done an internship in rehab I explained a very basic principle for listening under stress - when you notice the mood or the temperature of a conversation just went icy cold or red hot. I was fortunate to have been tutored in compassionate listening by The Venerable Pende Hawter, a Buddhist monk, who runs a palliative care hospice in Australia. That approach is available in a working document.

I was privileged to see how Cotton On in Australia decided to talk to their team through this crisis - a masterclass in integrity. The team have caught that ethos and importantly walk their talk.

But my client decided how they will talk to one another through this crisis - and I insisted they choose principles, values or guidelines that they were prepared to stick to, no matter what.

I think this approach is one of the secrets of Clear Sky Children's Charity. We have a very supportive and respectful way of engaging. While I am Chairman, I am also a team member and now more than ever, this compassionate leadership approach is working. The evidence is the continuity of services.

These are extraordinary times. As a charity we are receiving privileged updates to ensure that we are prepared. And we are prepared.

We are - all of us - are learning a lot right now. From my perspective, a silver lining of the pandemic is a definite change in the spirit of leadership. Crisis leadership.

I want to finish on this point. I wish it was my thinking but it is not.

From where I sit, the frontline is being manned primarily by women. The authentic leadership we need is being provided by women.

Jo Baldwin Trott - a contributor in this book - is a staunch advocate for more women leading, via her involvement in 5050 Parliament, points out that women have always been on the front-line of a crisis.

From where I sit the most engaged, yet the lowest paid workers. It appears that the leadership teams that fared better on the planet - faster and more effectively - were lead by women. It appears the governments driven by sharp egos, patronising bluster and agendas have experienced the harsh hand of reality.

I only hope that once the all-clear is sounded we don't forget these valuable insights and lessons. Can it be business as new normal?

I am proud to part of a team that does what it says on the tin. If you have been touched or inspired by my article please donate something to *www.clearskychildrenscharity.org* (UK).

Right now every little does help.

## About Andrew Priestley

Andrew Priestley mentors entrpre-neur leaders worldwide, is qualified in psychology, mentors leaders worldwide, is an award winning business coach, bestselling author and in demand speaker.

He is the Chairman of *Clear Sky Children's Charity UK* that provides support for vulnerable children aged 4-12 that have witnessed or directly experienced a trauma.

You can find him on LinkedIn or *www.andrewpriestley.com*

# Would You Like To Contribute To Future Editions Of Fit For Purpose Leadership?

If you would like to contribute to future editions of the *Fit For Purpose Leadership* series please contact *coachbiz@hotmail.com* and we will email you the Writers Guide.

Printed in Poland
by Amazon Fulfillment
Poland Sp. z o.o., Wrocław

57570841R00110